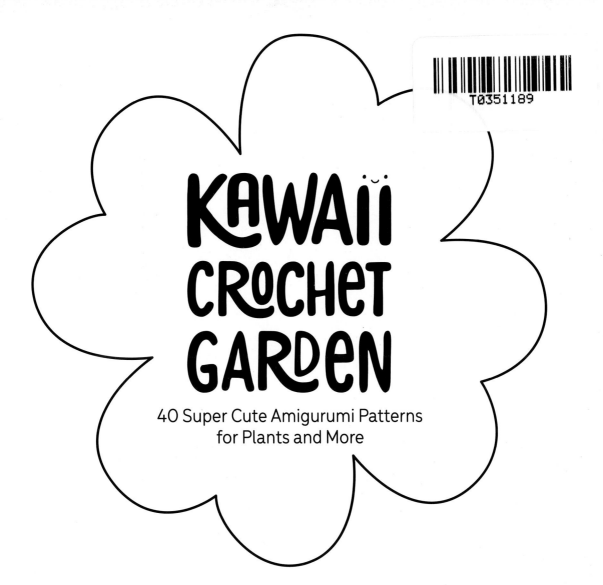

KAWAII CROCHET GARDEN

40 Super Cute Amigurumi Patterns
for Plants and More

Melissa Bradley

DAVID & CHARLES

www.davidandcharles.com

CONTENTS

Please refer to the Techniques section for guidance on any of the techniques used in this book.

INTRODUCTION

Just like my first book, *Kawaii Crochet*, this is a continued celebration of color—an ode to the natural phenomenon of the rainbow, a celebration of cute amigurumi crochet, and a reflection of the garden, all rolled into one.

I invite you to flip through the rainbow of chapters—pink, red, orange, yellow, green, blue, purple, and white. Immerse yourself in an adorable world of kawaii crochet. Learn something new about your favorite color, master a new technique in crocheting amigurumi, or simply enjoy making something adorably cute. Plus, pay special attention to the fun facts and puns sprinkled throughout the book, my personal invitation to go ahead and smile!

I hope this book brings you joy as it leads you through each color of the rainbow, and that the characters I have created bring a smile to your face and fill your heart with love as you stitch something handmade.

May we all discover a love for crochet, color, and all things cute!

Happy Crocheting!

Beginner   Easy   Intermediate

SKILL LEVELS

The level of difficulty for each project is indicated by one of three faces, which are shown here for your reference. If you're new to crochet, start with a Beginner or Easy project. Alternatively, if you're looking for more of a challenge, go for an Intermediate project.

TOOLS AND MATERIALS

CROCHET HOOKS

Size 3.5mm (US E/4) and 2.5mm (C/2). My favorites are Clover Amour crochet hooks; they are so comfy!

FIBERFILL STUFFING

Important for getting the right shape for your amigurumi. I use a polyester fiberfill stuffing.

STITCH MARKERS

With my stitch marker I always mark the last stitch of the round. Alternatively, use a piece of yarn in a contrast color, a safety pin, or a paper clip.

CHENILLE STEM (PIPE CLEANER)

Used instead of stuffing a flower stem with fiberfill and wire.

FLORAL WIRE

Green wire in a variety of thicknesses. I use 16-, 20-, and 26-gauge.

HOT GLUE GUN

My secret weapon when making amigurumi. When a pattern says "attach", that is when the hot glue gun gets plugged in! Now, a crochet purist would say...glue, no way! But I have found that when attaching bits and pieces to these kawaii characters, a hot glue gun is much faster and easier in the end. Of course, you can always use a needle and thread instead.

TOY SAFETY EYES

Black, sizes 5mm through 8mm, are what I use the most. Alternatively, use black yarn to embroider eyes (see Making Up: Inserting Safety Eyes).

SCISSORS

One of my favorite things to collect. They are best when they are pointy, sharp, and colorful!

YARN NEEDLE

This is a blunt needle and is essential for weaving in ends and shaping.

PINS

For keeping parts together. I like to use T-pins so that they don't get lost inside my amigurumi.

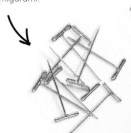

COTTON YARN

Two different yarn weights are used throughout this book and sometimes in the same pattern: Aran (worsted) and DK (light worsted).

WIRE CUTTERS

Resist the urge to use your scissors! Your hands (and scissors) will thank you later.

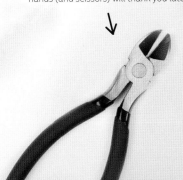

COLOR THEORY

Color influences us in so many ways! I have always felt a love for color, but my fascination with it really began in college when I took a class on color theory. Learning how color affects us was eye opening, and from that point on I found myself paying more attention to how I felt around certain colors. First, let's look at the terminology.

COLOR TERMS

PRIMARY COLORS

The color wheel is made up of three primary colors that cannot be made from any other colors. They are Red, Yellow, and Blue.

SECONDARY COLORS

These are Orange, Green, and Purple. They are created by mixing two primary colors together. Red + Yellow = Orange; Yellow + Blue = Green; Blue + Red = Purple.

TERTIARY COLORS

These are created by mixing one primary and one secondary color together. They include blue-green, yellow-green, yellow-orange, red-orange, red-purple, and blue-purple.

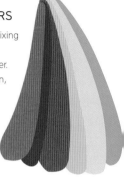

COMPLEMENTARY COLORS

Any two colors that are directly opposite each other on the color wheel are described as complementary colors—for example, red and green.

SPLIT-COMPLEMENTARY COLORS

These consist of any color on the wheel plus the two that flank its complement.

ANALAGOUS COLORS

These consist of any two to four colors which are side by side on the color wheel.

TRIADIC COLORS

These consist of any three colors evenly spaced around the color wheel.

TETRADIC OR DOUBLE COMPLEMENTARY COLORS

These consist of four colors arranged into two complementary pairs.

MONOCHROMATIC COLORS

These consist of one hue plus white, black, or gray to create tints, tones, and shades.

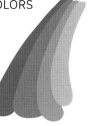

NEUTRAL COLORS

Colors that are not associated with any single hue, such as blacks, whites, and grays.

OTHER COLOR TERMS

HUE
The name of a color.

SATURATION
The intensity or purity of a hue.

VALUE
The degree of lightness or darkness of a hue. Also referred to as "tone".

SHADE
A hue produced by adding black.

TINT
A hue produced by adding white.

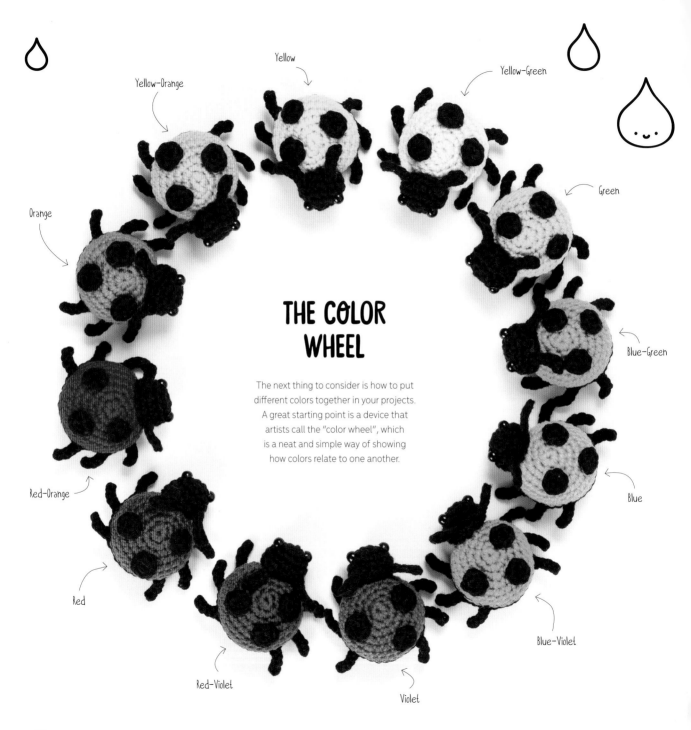

Yellow

Yellow-Orange

Yellow-Green

Green

Orange

Blue-Green

Red-Orange

Blue

Red

Blue-Violet

Red-Violet

Violet

THE COLOR WHEEL

The next thing to consider is how to put different colors together in your projects. A great starting point is a device that artists call the "color wheel", which is a neat and simple way of showing how colors relate to one another.

COLOR IN NATURE

The rainbow is nature's version of the color wheel. I believe that there are no ugly colors, only inappropriate combinations! So how do we choose colors that work harmoniously with other colors—and why do certain colors look better with other colors than on their own? The color wheel has all the answers to help us successfully pair colors.

Looking at the color wheel, you can quickly pick out a range of color combinations. These different color schemes guide your options between selecting contrasting or harmonious colors, depending on the effect you want to achieve.

Did you know that rainbows can exist at night? When light from the moon disperses through water droplets, the result is known as a moonbow. Because moonlight is fainter than sunlight, the bow may appear white, but a long-exposure camera can capture the full array of colors.

MONOCHROME COMBINATIONS

This kind of color scheme uses one hue (or color), plus white or black to create tints and shades. These combinations are great for simplifying and creating a harmonious, visually appealing look. For example, shades of blue always work well together—think of the sky meeting the ocean.

COMPLEMENTARY COMBINATIONS

Complementary colors—ones that are opposite each other on the color wheel—have high contrast to one another and, if used improperly, can be visually jarring. Generally speaking, you do not want to use equal amounts of complementary colors. Choose one of the hues as your main color, then use the complementary color to highlight it. These contrasting colors can be found in nature as well—for example, orange coral standing out in the blue of the ocean, or lavender against soft green foliage.

ANALOGOUS COMBINATIONS

These are any two to four colors that are side by side on the color wheel. I recommend that you choose a primary color as a base, then choose two more to highlight, not overwhelm. Be wary of choosing colors that are too closely related, as they may blend and wash out your design. Analogous color schemes are a common sight in nature. A popular example is the changing color of leaves in fall, yet analogous colors can be seen even in the petals of a single flower or in the sky at sunrise and sunset.

SPLIT COMPLEMENTARY COMBINATIONS

A split complementary color scheme comprises any color on the wheel plus the two that flank its complement—for example, blue with red-orange and yellow-orange. This strategy adds more variety, and results in combinations with both warm and cool hues that are more easily balanced than those of complementary color schemes. Because of this it is also good to remember which color in the combination is the strongest or the most dominant, because you do not want to create something that is busy rather than effective. In nature, an iris flower consisting of blue-purple, red-purple, and yellow is a good example of this color combination.

TRIADIC COMBINATIONS

These are any three colors that are evenly spaced around the color wheel. Triadic combinations tend to be quite vibrant, even when toned down, tinted or shaded, so choosing one main color and using the other two as accents is a strong place to start. The most basic triadic combination is red, yellow, and blue—for example, a clear blue sky meeting the red rock and yellow dry grass in a desert landscape.

TETRADIC COMBINATIONS

Like the triadic combination the tetradic involves colors that are equal distance apart; except these use four colors instead of three. These combinations are always loud and fun. However, caution must be used in finding balance with these combinations because they can be easily overwhelming. Green, yellow, red, and violet is a tetradic combination that can be found in a container of beautiful pansy flowers.

PiNK

The term "pink" derives from the garden pink (Dianthus), a small, sweet-smelling flower. However, in most European languages, the word for this color is rose or rosa, taken from the rose flower.

TULIP BULB

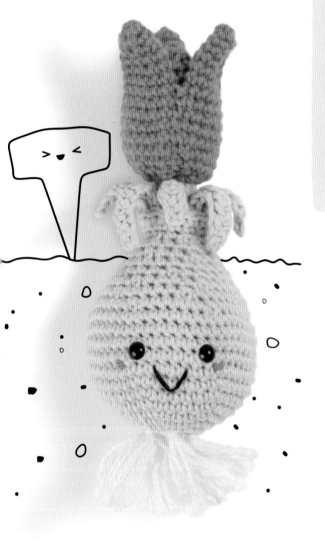

Materials

- 2.5mm (C/2) crochet hook
- Paintbox Yarns Cotton DK yarn: one 50g (1¾oz) ball each of Champagne White (**cream**), Light Caramel (**tan**), Lime Green (**lime green**), and Bubblegum Pink (**pink**)
- Scrap of **black** yarn
- 6mm safety eyes
- Fiberfill stuffing
- Yarn needle
- Stitch marker

Finished size

15cm (6in) tall by 6cm (2½in) wide

Gauge

6 sc sts and 7 rows = 2.5cm (1in)

BULB AND LEAVES

Rnd 1: with **cream** yarn, sc 6 in magic ring [6]

Rnd 2: 2 sc in each st around [12]

Rnd 3: change to **tan** yarn, (sc 1, 2 sc in next st) 6 times [18]

Rnd 4: (sc 2, 2 sc in next st) 6 times [24]

Rnd 5: (sc 3, 2 sc in next st) 6 times [30]

Rnd 6: (sc 4, 2 sc in next st) 6 times [36]

Rnd 7: (sc 5, 2 sc in next st) 6 times [42]

Rnd 8: (sc 6, 2 sc in next st) 6 times [48]

Rnds 9–13: sc in each st around [48]

Rnd 14: (sc 3, sc2tog, sc 3) 6 times [42]

Rnd 15: (sc2tog, sc 5) 6 times [36]

Rnd 16: (sc 2, sc2tog, sc 2) 6 times [30]

Place 6mm safety eyes between **Rnds 10 and 11**, with 5 sts in between. Begin to stuff with fiberfill.

Rnd 17: (sc2tog, sc 3) 6 times [24]

Rnd 18: sc in each st around [24]

Rnd 19: (sc 1, sc2tog, sc 1) 6 times [18]

Rnd 20: sc in each st around [18]

Rnd 21: (sc2tog, sc 1) 6 times [12]

Rnd 22: change to **lime green** yarn, working in BLO, sc in each st around [12]

Rnd 23: working in BLO, (sc2tog, sc 2) 3 times [9]

Rnds 24–26: sc in each st around [9]

Rnd 27: change to **pink** yarn, working in BLO, (sc 2, 2 sc in next st) 3 times [12]

Rnds 28–33: sc in each st around [12]

Rnd 34: (sc2tog, sc 4) 2 times [10]

Rnd 35: (sc2tog, sc 3) 2 times [8]

Rnd 36: (sc2tog, sc 2) 2 times [6]

Finish stuffing. Fasten off, leaving a long yarn tail. With a yarn needle, weave the tail through FLO to close the opening. Weave in all ends. Add stitches for the mouth and cheeks using **black** and **pink** yarn (see Making Up: Stitching Facial Details).

Rnd 37: join **lime green** yarn in any front loop from **Rnd 23**, (ch 8, sl st in 2nd ch from hook, sc 1, hdc 5, sl st in next 2 sts from **Rnd 23,** ch 10, sl st in 2nd ch from hook, sc 1, hdc 7, sl st in next st from **Rnd 23**) 3 times [6 leaves]

Fasten off and weave in ends.

Rnd 38: join **tan** yarn in any front loop from **Rnd 22**, (sc 3, 2 sc in next st) 3 times [15]

Rnd 39: sc in each st around [15]

Fasten off and weave in ends. Tie short lengths of **cream** yarn to **Rnds 1 and 2**. Cut them all the same length and unravel yarn to make it fuzzy.

TULIP PETAL (MAKE 3)

Rnd 1: with **pink** yarn, sc 4 in magic ring [4]

Rnd 2: (sc 1, 2 sc in next st) 2 times [6]

Rnd 3: (sc 2, 2 sc in next st) 2 times [8]

Rnd 4: (sc 3, 2 sc in next st) 2 times [10]

Rnd 5: (sc 4, 2 sc in next st) 2 times [12]

Rnd 6: sc in each st around [12]

Rnd 7: (sc 5, 2 sc in next st) 2 times [14]

Rnd 8: sc in each st around [14]

Rnd 9: (sc 6, 2 sc in next st) 2 times [16]

Rnd 10: sc in each st around [16]

Rnd 11: (sc 7, 2 sc in next st) 2 times [18]

Rnd 12: sc in each st around [18]

Rnd 13: (sc2tog, sc 1) 6 times [12]

Rnd 14: (sc2tog, sc 4) 2 times [10]

Fasten off, leaving a long yarn tail. Do not stuff with fiberfill but flatten. With yarn needle and yarn tail, sew **Rnd 14** together to close the opening. Sew **Rnd 14** of the petals to the front loops of **Rnd 26** of the bulb. Sew the sides of the petals together halfway up.

IS IT TULIP TO SAY I'M SORRY?

Did you know there's a secret language of flowers? Daisies mean "innocent or true love", sunflowers mean "love and admiration", and white tulips say "I'm sorry".

ROSE

Materials

- 3.5mm (E/4) crochet hook
- Paintbox Yarns Cotton Aran yarn: one 50g (1¾oz) ball each of Soft Fudge (**brown**), Ballet Pink (**light pink**), Bubblegum Pink (**pink**) and Grass Green (**green**)
- Scraps of **black** yarn
- 7mm safety eyes
- Fiberfill stuffing
- Yarn needle
- Stitch marker

Finished size

10cm (4in) tall by 7.5cm (3in) wide

Gauge

5 sc sts and 6 rows = 2.5cm (1in)

DIRT

Rnd 1: with **brown** yarn, sc 6 in magic ring [6]

Rnd 2: 2 sc in each st around [12]

Rnd 3: (sc 1, 2 sc in next st) 6 times [18]

Rnd 4: (sc 2, 2 sc in next st) 6 times [24]

Rnd 5: (sc 3, 2 sc in next st) 6 times [30]

Rnd 6: (sc 4, 2 sc in next st) 6 times [36]

Rnd 7: (sc 5, 2 sc in next st) 6 times [42]

Invisible fasten off (see Finishing: Invisible Fasten Off) and weave in ends.

POT

Rnd 1: with **light pink** yarn, sc 6 in magic ring [6]

Rnd 2: 2 sc in each st around [12]

Rnd 3: (sc 1, 2 sc in next st) 6 times [18]

Rnd 4: (sc 2, 2 sc in next st) 6 times [24]

Rnd 5: (sc 3, 2 sc in next st) 6 times [30]

Rnd 6: (sc 4, 2 sc in next st) 6 times [36]

Rnd 7: working in BLO, sc in each st around [36]

Rnds 8–11: sc in each st around [36]

Rnd 12: (sc 5, 2 sc in next st) 6 times [42]

Rnds 13–15: sc in each st around [42]

Place 7mm safety eyes between **Rnds 11 and 12**, with 4 sts in between. Begin to stuff with fiberfill. Do not fasten off and cut yarn.

Rnd 16: place dirt in pot and line up stitches from **Rnd 15** of pot and **Rnd 7** of dirt. With **light pink** yarn, sc in each st around working in both loops of both pieces to join them together (see Making Up: Crocheting Two Pieces Together) [42]

Rnd 17: ch 1, sc in each st around, join with sl st in first st [42]

Rnd 18: sl st in each st around [42]

Invisible fasten off and weave in ends. Stitch on mouth and cheeks using **black** and **pink** yarn (see Making Up: Stitching Facial Details). Begin shaping by inserting needle from center bottom to center top, then insert needle back down from center top to slightly off center bottom. Insert needle from center bottom to center top. Pull to create an indentation in bottom of pot. Fasten off and weave in ends.

ROSE

Rnd 1: with **pink** yarn, ch 53, dc in 5th ch from hook, (ch 1, skip next ch st, dc + ch 1 + dc in next ch st) to end of row, turn [50]

Rnd 2: ch 2, (hdc + 4 dc + hdc in next ch-1 space, sl st in next ch-1 space) 24 times. Do not work in last ch-space [24 petals]

Fasten off, leaving a 30cm (12in) tail. Roll loosely into a rose shape. Sew rose together on back side using yarn tail and a yarn needle (1). Attach to top center of dirt.

LEAF (MAKE 2)

Rnd 1: with **green** yarn, ch 10, sl st in 2nd ch from hook, sc 1, hdc 1, dc 4, hdc 1, sc 3, turn to work on other side of foundation ch, hdc 1, dc 4, hdc 1, sc 1, sl st 1, sl st in beginning skipped ch st [20]

Invisible fasten off and weave in ends. Attach to dirt under rose.

Leaf Chart

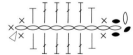

LiLY

Materials

- 3.5mm (E/4) and 2.5mm (C/2) crochet hooks
- Paintbox Yarns Cotton Aran yarn: one 50g (1¾oz) ball each of Ballet Pink (**light pink**) and Washed Teal (**blue**)
- Paintbox Yarns Cotton DK yarn: one 50g (1¾oz) ball each of Raspberry Pink (**dark pink**), Bubblegum Pink (**pink**), and Ballet Pink (**light pink**), and Grass Green (**green**)
- Scrap of **black** yarn
- 7mm safety eyes
- Fiberfill stuffing
- Chenille stem (pipe cleaner)
- Yarn needle
- Stitch marker

Finished size

21.5cm (8½in) tall by 10cm (4in) wide

Gauge

5 sc sts and 6 rows = 2.5cm (1in) using Aran yarn

6 sc sts and 7 rows = 2.5cm (1in) using DK yarn

BUD VASE

Rnd 1: with **3.5mm** hook and **light pink** Aran yarn, sc 6 in magic ring [6]

Rnd 2: 2 sc in each st around [12]

Rnd 3: (sc 1, 2 sc in next st) 6 times [18]

Rnd 4: (sc 2, 2 sc in next st) 6 times [24]

Rnd 5: (sc 3, 2 sc in next st) 6 times [30]

Rnd 6: working in BLO, sc in each st around [30]

Rnd 7: (sc 4, 2 sc in next st) 6 times [36]

Rnds 8–9: sc in each st around [36]

Rnd 10: (sc 5, 2 sc in next st) 6 times [42]

Rnds 11–13: sc in each st around [42]

Rnd 14: (sc2tog, sc 5) 6 times [36]

Rnd 15: (sc2tog, sc 4) 6 times [30]

Rnd 16: (sc2tog, sc 3) 6 times [24]

Rnd 17: (sc2tog, sc 6) 3 times [21]

Place 7mm safety eyes between **Rnds 11 and 12**, with 4 sts in between. Stuff with fiberfill. Do not finish off and cut yarn. Make the water before moving on to **Rnd 18**.

Rnd 18: place the water in the vase and line up the stitches from **Rnd 17** of the vase and **Rnd 4** of the water. With the yarn used to make the vase, sc in each st around, working in both loops of both pieces to join them together (see Making Up: Crocheting Two Pieces Together) [21]

Rnds 19–29: sc in each st around [21]

Rnd 30: sl st in each st around [21]

Invisible fasten off (see Finishing: Invisible Fasten Off) and weave in ends. Add stitches for the mouth and cheeks using **black** and **pink** yarn (see Making Up: Stitching Facial Details).

Begin shaping by inserting needle from center bottom to center top, take needle back down from center top to slightly off center bottom and back up to center top. Pull to create an indentation in the bottom of the vase. Fasten off and weave in ends.

WATER

Rnd 1: with **3.5mm** hook and **blue Aran** yarn, sc 6 in magic ring [6]

Rnd 2: 2 sc in each st around [12]

Rnd 3: (sc 1, 2 sc in next st) 6 times [18]

Rnd 4: (sc 5, 2 sc in next st) 3 times [21]

Invisible fasten off and weave in ends.

LILY (MAKE 2)

Rnd 1: with **2.5mm** hook and **dark pink DK** yarn, sc 15 in magic ring [15]

Rnd 2: ch 12, sc in 2nd ch from hook, sc 10, ch 2, working on the other side of the foundation ch, sc 1, hdc 1, dc 1, 2 dc in next st, dc 1, hdc 2, sc 3, 3 sc in last st [25]

Rnd 3: sc 4, hdc 2, dc 1, 2 dc in next st, dc 1, hdc 1, sc 1, 3 sc in ch-2 space, change to **pink DK** yarn, sc 13, 3 hdc in next st [33]

Rnd 4: sc 12, change to **dark pink DK** yarn, skip next 2 sts in magic ring, sl st 3 [15]

Rnds 5–10: repeat **Rnds 2–4** twice, fasten off and weave in ends

Rnd 11: change to **light pink DK** yarn, sc around entire lily, making a sc + hdc + ch 2 + hdc + sc at the top of each petal

Fasten off and weave in ends.

STEM

Rnd 1: With **2.5mm** hook and **green DK** yarn, sc 5 in magic ring [5]

Rnds 2–20: sc in each st around [5]

Rnd 21: (working in back bump sts, ch 7, sl st in 2nd ch from hook, sl st 5, working in FLO, sl st 1 in next unworked st from **Rnd 20**) 3 times [35]

Fasten off, leaving a long yarn tail. Do not stuff with fiberfill. With yarn needle, weave tail through BLO to close the opening. Insert chenille stem through **Rnd 1** of stem, leaving 2.5cm (1in) extending beyond the stem. Push both flower elements from below onto the stem (1).

LEAF (MAKE 5)

Rnd 1: with **2.5mm** hook and **green DK** yarn, ch 12, sl st in 2nd ch from hook, sc 1, hdc 2, dc 4, hdc 2, sc 3, working on the other side of the foundation ch, hdc 2, dc 4, hdc 2, sc 1, sl st 1, sl st in beginning skipped ch st [24]

Invisible fasten off and weave in ends.

Attach the leaves to the stem (2).

Insert the lily into the bud vase.

Leaf Chart

COLEUS

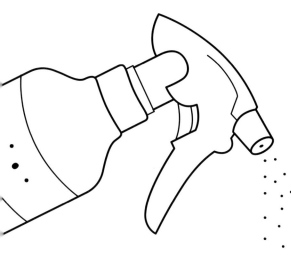

Materials

- 3.5mm (E/4) and 2.5mm (C/2) crochet hooks
- Paintbox Yarns Cotton Aran yarn: one 50g (1¾oz) ball each of Bubblegum Pink (**pink**), Champagne White (**cream**) and Soft Fudge (**brown**)
- Paintbox Yarns Cotton DK yarn: one 50g (1¾oz) ball each of Bubblegum Pink (**pink**), and Raspberry Pink (**dark pink**), and Lime Green (**lime green**)
- Scraps of **black** and **pink** yarn
- 8mm safety eyes
- Fiberfill stuffing
- Yarn needle
- Stitch marker

Finished size

12.5cm (5in) tall by 12.5cm (5in) wide

Gauge

5 sc sts and 6 rows = 2.5cm (1in) using Aran yarn

6 sc sts and 7 rows = 2.5cm (1in) using DK yarn

POT

Rnd 1: with **3.5mm** hook and **pink Aran** yarn, sc 6 in magic ring [6]

Rnd 2: 2 sc in each st around [12]

Rnd 3: (sc 1, 2 sc in next st) 6 times [18]

Rnd 4: (sc 2, 2 sc in next st) 6 times [24]

Rnd 5: (sc 3, 2 sc in next st) 6 times [30]

Rnd 6: (sc 4, 2 sc in next st) 6 times [36]

Rnd 7: (sc 5, 2 sc in next st) 6 times [42]

Rnd 8: working in BLO, sc in each st around [42]

Rnds 9–13: sc in each st around [42]

Rnd 14: (sc 6, 2 sc in next st) 6 times [48]

Rnd 15: sc in each st around [48]

Rnd 16: change to **cream Aran** yarn, sc in each st around [48]

Rnd 17: sc in each st around [48]

Place 8mm safety eyes between **Rnds 13 and 14**, with 5 sts in between. Begin to stuff with fiberfill. Do not finish off and cut yarn. Make the dirt before moving on to **Rnd 18**.

Rnd 18: place the dirt in the pot and line up the stitches from **Rnd 17** of the pot and **Rnd 8** of the dirt. With the yarn used to make the pot, sc in each st around, working in both loops of both pieces to join them together (see Making Up: Crocheting Two Pieces Together) [48]

Rnd 19: ch 1, sc in each st around, join with sl st in first st [48]

Rnd 20: sl st in each st around [48]

Invisible fasten off (see Finishing: Invisible Fasten Off) and weave in ends. Add stitches for the mouth and cheeks, using **black** and **pink** yarn (see Making Up: Stitching Facial Details).

Begin shaping by inserting needle from center bottom to center top, then take needle back down from center top to slightly off center bottom and back up to center top. Pull to create an indentation in the bottom of the pot. Fasten off and weave in ends.

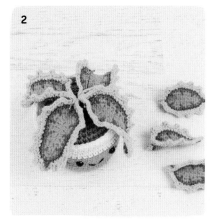

DIRT

Rnd 1: with **3.5mm** hook and **brown Aran** yarn, sc 6 in magic ring [6]

Rnd 2: 2 sc in each st around [12]

Rnd 3: (sc 1, 2 sc in next st) 6 times [18]

Rnd 4: (sc 2, 2 sc in next st) 6 times [24]

Rnd 5: (sc 3, 2 sc in next st) 6 times [30]

Rnd 6: (sc 4, 2 sc in next st) 6 times [36]

Rnd 7: (sc 5, 2 sc in next st) 6 times [42]

Rnd 8: (sc 6, 2 sc in next st) 6 times [48]

Invisible fasten off and weave in ends.

LARGE LEAF (MAKE 4)

Rnd 1: with **2.5mm** hook and **pink DK** yarn, ch 12, sc in 2nd ch from hook, hdc 1, dc 1, 2 dc in next ch st, dc 2, hdc 2, sc 2, 3 sc in last ch st, working on the other side of the foundation ch, sc 2, hdc 2, dc 2, 2 dc in next st, dc 1, hdc 1, sc 1 [25]

Rnd 2: sc 2, 2 sc in next 3 sts, sc 7, 3 sc in next st, sc 7, 2 sc in next 3 sts, sc 2 [33]

Rnd 3: change to **dark pink DK** yarn, sc 4, (sc + scSP-1, sc 2) 4 times, sc + ch 3 + sc in 2nd and 3rd ch sts, sc 3, (sc + scSP-1, sc 2) 4 times, sc 1 [43 sc sts]

Rnd 4: change to **lime green DK** yarn, sc 5, (sc + ch 3 + sc, sc 2) 6 times, ch 3, sc 2, (sc + ch 3 + sc, sc 2) 6 times, sc 2 [57]

Sl st in next st, invisible fasten off, and weave in ends.

Pinch the base of each leaf and glue or sew together (1).

Attach the leaves to the dirt, spacing them evenly (2).

MEDIUM LEAF (MAKE 4)

Rnd 1: with **2.5mm** hook and **pink DK** yarn, ch 9, sc in 2nd ch from hook, hdc 1, 2 dc in next ch st, hdc 2, sc 2, 3 sc in last ch st, working on the other side of the foundation ch, sc 2, hdc 2, 2 dc in next st, hdc 1, sc 1 [19]

Rnd 2: sc 2, 2 sc in next 2 sts, sc 5, 3 sc in next st, sc 5, 2 sc in next 2 sts, sc 2 [25]

Rnd 3: change to **dark pink DK** yarn, sc 3, (sc + scSP-1, sc 2) 3 times, sc + ch 3 + sc in 2nd and 3rd ch sts, sc 2, (sc + scSP-1, sc 2) 3 times, sc 1 [33 sc sts]

Rnd 4: change to **lime green DK** yarn, sc 4, (sc + ch 3 + sc, sc 2) 4 times, ch 3, sc 4, (sc + ch 3 + sc, sc 2) 4 times, sc 1 [43]

Sl st in next st, invisible fasten off, and weave in ends. Pinch the base of each leaf and glue or sew together. Space the medium leaves evenly in between the large leaves and attach them to the large leaves (3).

SMALL LEAF (MAKE 2)

Rnd 1: with **2.5mm** hook and **pink DK** yarn, ch 9, sc in 2nd ch from hook, hdc 1, 2 dc in next ch st, hdc 2, sc 2, 3 sc in last ch st, working on the other side of the foundation ch, sc 2, hdc 2, 2 dc in next st, hdc 1, sc 1 [19]

Rnd 2: change to **dark pink DK** yarn, sc 1, (sc + scSP-1, sc 2) 2 times, sc + scSP-1, sc 1, sc + ch 3 + sc in 2nd and 3rd ch sts, sc 1, (sc + scSP-1, sc 2) 2 times, sc + scSP-1, sc 1 [27 sc sts]

Rnd 3: change to **lime green DK** yarn, sc 3, (sc + ch 3 + sc, sc 2) 3 times, (sc + ch 3 + sc, sc 2 in loops of ch from Rnd 2), ch 3, sc 2, (sc + ch 3 + sc, sc 2) 4 times [37]

Sl st in next st, invisible fasten off, and weave in ends. Pinch the base of each leaf and glue or sew together. Space the small leaves evenly in between the medium leaves and attach them to the medium leaves (4).

3

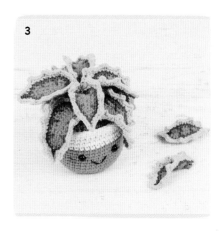

4

WORM

Materials

- 2.5mm (C/2) crochet hook
- Paintbox Yarns Cotton DK yarn:
  one 50g (1¾oz) ball each of
  Bubblegum Pink (**pink**) and
  Peach Orange (**peach**)
- 5mm safety eyes
- Fiberfill stuffing
- 20-gauge floral wire
- Yarn needle
- Stitch marker

Finished size

5cm (2in) tall by
12.5cm (5in) wide

Gauge

6 sc sts and 7 rows
= 2.5cm (1in)

WORM

Rnd 1: with **pink** yarn, sc 6 in magic ring [6]

Rnd 2: 2 sc in each st around [12]

Rnd 3: (sc 1, 2 sc in next st) 6 times [18]

Rnds 4–7: sc in each st around [18]

Place 5mm safety eyes between **Rnds 4 and 5**, with 3 sts in between. Begin to stuff with fiberfill.

Rnd 8: sc 5, (sc2tog) 4 times, sc 5 [14]

Rnd 9: sc 3, (sc2tog) 4 times, sc 3 [10]

Rnd 10: sc in each st around [10]

Rnd 11: change to **peach** yarn,
sc in each st around [10]

Rnd 12: change to **pink** yarn,
sc in each st around [10]

Rnds 13–16: sc in each st around [10]

Rnd 17: change to **peach** yarn,
sc in each st around [10]

Rnds 18–35: repeat **Rnds 12–17**

Rnd 36: change to **pink** yarn,
sc in each st around [10]

Rnd 37: sc in each st around [10]

Rnd 38: (sc2tog, sc 3) 2 times [8]

Rnd 39: sc in each st around [8]

Rnd 40: (sc2tog, sc 2) 2 times [6]

Finish stuffing. Insert floral wire the length of the worm. Fasten off, leaving a long yarn tail. With a yarn needle, weave the tail through FLO to close the opening. Weave in all ends. Bend the worm into a wiggly shape.

RED

Red represents magic in nearly every culture, so it is not surprising that garden gnomes traditionally wear red hats. For centuries, the color red has been used in gardens to add flavor and emotion.

CHRISTMAS CACTUS

Materials

- 3.5mm (E/4) and 2.5mm (C/2) crochet hooks
- Paintbox Yarns Cotton Aran yarn: one 50g (1¾oz) ball each of Pillar Red (**red**) and Soft Fudge (**brown**)
- Paintbox Yarns Cotton DK yarn: one 50g (1¾oz) ball each of Spearmint Green (**green**) and Pillar Red (**red**)
- Scraps of **black** and **pink** yarn
- 8mm safety eyes
- Fiberfill stuffing
- 26-gauge floral wire
- Yarn needle
- Stitch marker

Finished size

19cm (7½in) tall by 18cm (7in) wide

Gauge

5 sc sts and 6 rows = 2.5cm (1in) using Aran yarn

6 sc sts and 7 rows = 2.5cm (1in) using DK yarn

POT

Rnd 1: with **3.5mm** hook and **red Aran** yarn, sc 6 in magic ring [6]

Rnd 2: 2 sc in each st around [12]

Rnd 3: (sc 1, 2 sc in next st) 6 times [18]

Rnd 4: (sc 2, 2 sc in next st) 6 times [24]

Rnd 5: (sc 3, 2 sc in next st) 6 times [30]

Rnd 6: (sc 4, 2 sc in next st) 6 times [36]

Rnd 7: (sc 5, 2 sc in next st) 6 times [42]

Rnd 8: working in BLO, sc in each st around [42]

Rnds 9–13: sc in each st around [42]

Rnd 14: (sc 6, 2 sc in next st) 6 times [48]

Rnds 15–17: sc in each st around [48]

Place 8mm safety eyes between **Rnds 13 and 14**, with 5 sts in between. Begin to stuff with fiberfill. Do not finish off and cut yarn. Make the dirt before moving on to **Rnd 18**.

Rnd 18: place the dirt in the pot and line up the stitches from **Rnd 17** of the pot and **Rnd 8** of the dirt. With the yarn used to make the pot, sc in each st around, working in both loops of both pieces to join them together (see Making Up: Crocheting Two Pieces Together) [48]

Rnd 19: ch 1, sc in each st around, join with sl st in first st [48]

Rnd 20: sl st in each st around [48]

Invisible fasten off (see Finishing: Invisible Fasten Off) and weave in ends. Add stitches for the mouth and cheeks using black and pink yarn (see Making Up: Stitching Facial Details).

Begin shaping by inserting needle from center bottom to center top, then take needle back down from center top to slightly off center bottom and back up to center top. Pull to create an indentation in the bottom of the pot. Fasten off and weave in ends.

DIRT

Rnd 1: with **3.5mm** hook and **brown Aran** yarn, sc 6 in magic ring [6]

Rnd 2: 2 sc in each st around [12]

Rnd 3: (sc 1, 2 sc in next st) 6 times [18]

Rnd 4: (sc 2, 2 sc in next st) 6 times [24]

Rnd 5: (sc 3, 2 sc in next st) 6 times [30]

Rnd 6: (sc 4, 2 sc in next st) 6 times [36]

Rnd 7: (sc 5, 2 sc in next st) 6 times [42]

Rnd 8: (sc 6, 2 sc in next st) 6 times [48]

Invisible fasten off and weave in ends.

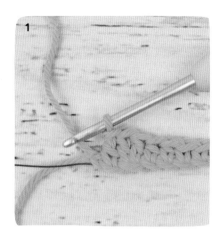

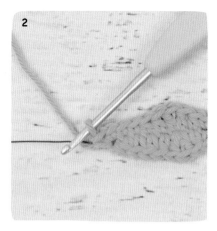

WE WISH YOU A MERRY CACTUS...

Wondering how this cactus got its name? It's simply due to its blooming time, which coincides with Christian holiday traditions.

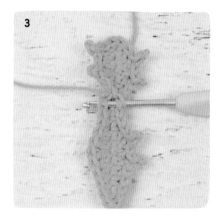

STEM (MAKE 9)

Rnd 1: with **2.5mm** hook and **green DK** yarn, ch 16, cut a 15cm (6in) piece of floral wire, hold behind the foundation ch and crochet the following sts around the wire (see Making Up: Crocheting with Floral Wire): sc in 2nd ch from hook, sc 1, hdc 2, 2 dc in next st, hdc 1, sc 4, hdc 2, 2 dc in next st, hdc 1 (1), bend wire end behind sts, 3 sc in last st, working on the other side of the foundation ch, hdc 1, 2 dc in next st, hdc 2, sc 4, hdc 1, 2 dc in next st, hdc 2, sc 2, 2 sc in beginning skipped ch st (2) [37]

Rnd 2: sl st 4, ch-2 picot, sl st 2, ch-2 picot, sl st 7, ch-2 picot, sl st 2, ch-2 picot, sl st 5, ch-2 picot, sl st 2, ch-2 picot, sl st 3, sl st both sides of stem together by first inserting hook on the opposite side and then in the next st on the current side of the stem (3), sl st 3, ch-2 picot, sl st 2, ch-2 picot, sl st 6 [45]

Fasten off, leaving a long yarn tail for sewing the stem to the dirt.

BLOSSOM (MAKE 9)

Rnd 1: with **2.5mm** hook and **red DK** yarn, sc 6 in magic ring [6]

Rnd 2: sc in each st around [6]

Rnd 3: (ch 3, hdc + dc + hdc in 3rd ch from hook, working in FLO, sc 2) 3 times [15]

Rnd 4: working in BLO from **Rnd 2**, sc in each st around [6]

Rnd 5: sc in each st around [6]

Rnd 6: (ch 3, hdc + dc + hdc in 3rd ch from hook, sc 2) 3 times [15]

Fasten off and weave in ends.

Attach a blossom to the end of each stem (4).

Push three stems into the center of the dirt and sew them to the dirt with yarn needle and yarn tail. Next, push six stems in a circle around the first three stems and sew in place. Bend the stems into a droopy position.

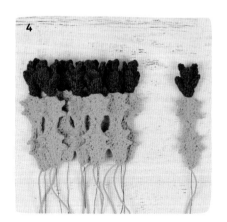

LADYBUG

Materials

- 2.5mm (C/2) crochet hook
- Paintbox Yarns Cotton DK yarn: one 50g (1¾oz) ball each of Pure Black (**black**) and Pillar Red (**red**)
- 6mm safety eyes
- Fiberfill stuffing
- Yarn needle
- Stitch marker

Finished size

2.5cm (1in) tall by 7.5cm (3in) wide

Gauge

6 sc sts and 7 rows = 2.5cm (1in)

TOP PIECE

Rnd 1: with **red** yarn, sc 6 in magic ring [6]

Rnd 2: 2 sc in each st around [12]

Rnd 3: (sc 1, 2 sc in next st) 6 times [18]

Rnd 4: (sc 2, 2 sc in next st) 6 times [24]

Rnd 5: (sc 3, 2 sc in next st) 6 times [30]

Rnds 6-8: sc in each st around [30]

Fasten off and weave in ends.

BOTTOM PIECE

Rnd 1: with **black** yarn, sc 6 in magic ring [6]

Rnd 2: 2 sc in each st around [12]

Rnd 3: (sc 1, 2 sc in next st) 6 times [18]

Rnd 4: (sc 2, 2 sc in next st) 6 times [24]

Rnd 5: (sc 3, 2 sc in next st) 6 times [30]

Begin to stuff with fiberfill.

Rnd 6: place top piece under bottom piece, lining up stitches from **Rnd 8** of top piece and **Rnd 5** of bottom piece. With **black** yarn and working in BLO of both pieces to join them together to form body, sl st 4, (sl st + ch 5 + sl st in 2nd ch from hook + sl st in next 3 ch sts + sl st, sl st 2) 3 times, sl st 6, (sl st + ch 5 + sl st in 2nd ch from hook + sl st in next 3 ch sts + sl st, sl st 2) 3 times, sl st 2 [60]

Finish stuffing with fiberfill. Fasten off and weave in ends.

SPOTS (MAKE 3)

Rnd 1: with **black** yarn, sc 6 in magic ring, sl st in first st to join [6]

Fasten off and attach to body.

ANTENNA (MAKE 2)

Rnd 1: with **black** yarn, ch 6, working in back bump loops, sc in 2nd ch from hook, sl st in next 4 ch sts [5]

Fasten off, leaving a long yarn tail.

HEAD

Rnd 1: with **black** yarn, sc 5 in magic ring [5]

Rnd 2: 2 sc in each st around [10]

Rnd 3: (sc 1, 2 sc in next st) 5 times [15]

Rnds 4-5: sc in each st around [15]

Place 6mm safety eyes between **Rnds 2 and 3**, with 4 sts in between. Attach antennae between **Rnds 4 and 5** directly above the eyes. Begin to stuff with fiberfill.

Rnd 6: working in BLO, (sc 1, sc2tog) 5 times [10]

Rnd 7: (sc2tog) 5 times [5]

Finish stuffing. Fasten off, leaving a long tail. With a yarn needle, weave tail through FLO to close opening. Weave in ends. Attach head to front of body.

POINSETTIA

Materials

- 3.5mm (E/4) and 2.5mm (C/2) crochet hooks
- Paintbox Yarns Cotton Aran yarn: one 50g (1¾oz) ball each of Vanilla Cream (**cream**) and Soft Fudge (**brown**)
- Paintbox Paintbox Yarns Cotton DK yarn: one 50g (1¾oz) ball each of Pillar Red (**red**), Racing Green (**dark green**), and Buttercup Yellow (**yellow**)
- Scrap of **black** yarn
- 7mm safety eyes
- Fiberfill stuffing
- Yarn needle
- Stitch marker

Finished size

10cm (4in) tall by 7.5cm (3in) wide

Gauge

5 sc sts and 6 rows = 2.5cm (1in) using Aran yarn

6 sc sts and 7 rows = 2.5cm (1in) using DK yarn

POT

Rnd 1: with **3.5mm** hook and **cream Aran** yarn, sc 6 in magic ring [6]

Rnd 2: 2 sc in each st around [12]

Rnd 3: (sc 1, 2 sc in next st) 6 times [18]

Rnd 4: (sc 2, 2 sc in next st) 6 times [24]

Rnd 5: (sc 3, 2 sc in next st) 6 times [30]

Rnd 6: (sc 4, 2 sc in next st) 6 times [36]

Rnd 7: working in BLO, sc in each st around [36]

Rnds 8–11: sc in each st around [36]

Rnd 12: (sc 5, 2 sc in next st) 6 times [42]

Rnds 13–15: sc in each st around [42]

Place 7mm safety eyes between **Rnds 11 and 12**, with 4 sts in between. Begin to stuff with fiberfill. Do not finish off and cut yarn. Make the dirt before moving on to **Rnd 16**.

Rnd 16: place the dirt in the pot and line up the stitches from **Rnd 15** of the pot and **Rnd 7** of the dirt. With the yarn used to make the pot, sc in each st around, working in both loops of both pieces to join them together (see Making Up: Crocheting Two Pieces Together) [42]

Rnd 17: ch 1, sc in each st around, join with sl st in first st [42]

Rnd 18: sl st in each st around [42]

Invisible fasten off (see Finishing: Invisible Fasten Off) and weave in ends. Add stitches for the mouth and cheeks using **black** and **red** yarn (see Making Up: Stitching Facial Details). Begin shaping by inserting needle from center bottom to center top, then take needle back down from center top to slightly off center bottom and back up to center top. Pull to create an indentation in the bottom of the pot. Fasten off and weave in ends.

DIRT

Rnd 1: with **3.5mm** hook and **brown Aran** yarn, sc 6 in magic ring [6]

Rnd 2: 2 sc in each st around [12]

Rnd 3: (sc 1, 2 sc in next st) 6 times [18]

Rnd 4: (sc 2, 2 sc in next st) 6 times [24]

Rnd 5: (sc 3, 2 sc in next st) 6 times [30]

Rnd 6: (sc 4, 2 sc in next st) 6 times [36]

Rnd 7: (sc 5, 2 sc in next st) 6 times [42]

Invisible fasten off and weave in ends.

SMALL PETAL (MAKE 6)

Rnd 1: with **2.5mm** hook and **red DK** yarn, sc 4 in magic ring [4]

Rnd 2: (sc 1, 2 sc in next st) 2 times [6]

Rnd 3: (sc 2, 2 sc in next st) 2 times [8]

Rnd 4: (sc 3, 2 sc in next st) 2 times [10]

Rnd 5: (sc 4, 2 sc in next st) 2 times [12]

Rnds 6–7: sc in each st around [12]

Rnd 8: (sc2tog, sc 4) 2 times [10]

Rnd 9: (sc2tog, sc 3) 2 times [8]

Sl st in next st. Fasten off, leaving a long tail. Do not stuff with fiberfill stuffing. Flatten and sew opening closed with a yarn needle and yarn tail, then sew the two sides together. Using a yarn tail from one of the petals, sew all six petals together in a circle (1).

CENTER

Rnd 1: with **2.5mm hook** and **yellow DK** yarn, sc 6 in magic ring [6]

Rnd 2: working in FLO, 5 sc in each st around [30]

Rnd 3: working in BLO from **Rnd 1**, (2 sc + ch 2 + 2 sc in next st) 6 times [36]

Fasten off and weave in ends

LARGE PETAL (MAKE 4 RED AND 2 GREEN)

Rnd 1: with **2.5mm** hook and DK yarn in the appropriate color, sc 4 in magic ring [4]

Rnd 2: (sc 1, 2 sc in next st) 2 times [6]

Rnd 3: (sc 2, 2 sc in next st) 2 times [8]

Rnd 4: (sc 3, 2 sc in next st) 2 times [10]

Rnd 5: (sc 4, 2 sc in next st) 2 times [12]

Rnd 6: (sc 5, 2 sc in next st) 2 times [14]

Rnds 7–8: sc in each st around [14]

Rnd 9: (sc2tog, sc 5) 2 times [12]

Rnd 10: (sc2tog, sc 4) 2 times [10]

Rnd 11: (sc2tog, sc 3) 2 times [8]

Sl st in next st. Fasten off, leaving a long tail. Do not stuff with fiberfill stuffing. Flatten and sew opening closed with a yarn needle and yarn tail, then sew the two sides together. Make a total of six petals—four with **red** yarn and two with **dark green** yarn.

Using a yarn tail from one of the petals, sew all six petals together in a circle (2).

Attach the circle of large petals to the dirt.

Attach the circle of small petals to the top of the large petals.

Attach the center to the circle of small petals (3).

POPPY

Materials

- 3.5mm (E/4) and 2.5mm (C/2) crochet hooks
- Paintbox Yarns Cotton Aran yarn: one 50g (1¾oz) ball each of Champagne White (**cream**) and Washed Teal (**blue**)
- Paintbox Yarns Cotton DK yarn: one 50g (1¾oz) ball each of Pillar Red (**red**), Buttercup Yellow (**yellow**), Pure Black (**black**), and Grass Green (**green**)
- Scraps of **black** and **pink** yarn
- 7mm safety eyes
- Fiberfill stuffing
- 16-gauge floral wire
- Yarn needle
- Stitch marker

Finished size

16.5cm (6½in) tall by 9cm (3½in) wide

Gauge

5 sc sts and 6 rows = 2.5cm (1in) using Aran yarn

6 sc sts and 7 rows = 2.5cm (1in) using DK yarn

VASE

Rnd 1: with **3.5mm** hook and **cream Aran** yarn, sc 6 in magic ring [6]

Rnd 2: 2 sc in each st around [12]

Rnd 3: (sc 1, 2 sc in next st) 6 times [18]

Rnd 4: (sc 2, 2 sc in next st) 6 times [24]

Rnd 5: (sc 3, 2 sc in next st) 6 times [30]

Rnd 6: (sc 4, 2 sc in next st) 6 times [36]

Rnd 7: working in BLO, sc in each st around [36]

Rnd 8: sc in each st around [36]

Rnd 9: (sc 5, 2 sc in next st) 6 times [42]

Rnds 10–16: sc in each st around [42]

Rnd 17: (sc2tog, sc 5) 6 times [36]

Rnd 18: (sc 2, sc2tog, sc 2) 6 times [30]

Rnd 19: (sc2tog, sc 3) 6 times [24]

Place 7mm safety eyes between **Rnds 11 and 12**, with 4 sts in between. Stuff with fiberfill. Do not finish off and cut yarn. Make the water before moving on to **Rnd 20**.

Rnd 20: place the water in the vase and line up the stitches from **Rnd 19** of the vase and **Rnd 4** of the water. With the yarn used to make the vase, sc in each st around, working in both loops of both pieces to join them together (see Making Up: Crocheting Two Pieces Together) [24]

Rnds 21–22: sc in each st around [24]

Rnd 23: (sc 3, 2 sc in next st) 6 times [30]

Rnds 24–25: sc in each st around [30]

Rnd 26: sl st in each st around [30]

Invisible fasten off (see Finishing: Invisible Fasten Off) and weave in ends. Add stitches for the mouth and cheeks, using **black** and **pink** yarn (see Making Up: Stitching Facial Details). Begin shaping by inserting needle from center bottom to center top, then take needle back down from center top to slightly off center bottom and back up to center top. Pull to create an indentation in the bottom of the vase. Fasten off and weave in ends.

WATER

Rnd 1: with **3.5mm** hook and **blue Aran** yarn, sc 6 in magic ring [6]

Rnd 2: 2 sc in each st around [12]

Rnd 3: (sc 1, 2 sc in next st) 6 times [18]

Rnd 4: (sc 2, 2 sc in next st) 6 times [24]

Invisible fasten off and weave in ends.

POPPY (MAKE 6)

Rnd 1: with **2.5mm** hook and **red DK** yarn, sc 8 in magic ring [8]

Rnd 2: 2 sc in each st around [16]

You will now be working in rows to complete each petal.

Row 3: working in FLO, sc 4, turn [4]

Row 4: ch 1, 2 sc in next st, sc2tog, 2 sc in next st, turn [5]

Row 5: ch 1, 2 sc in next st, sc 3, 2 sc in next st, turn [7]

Row 6: ch 1, 2 sc in next st, sc 5, 2 sc in next st, turn [9]

Row 7: sc in each st across [9]

Row 8: sl st down the left side of petal [5]

Repeat **Rows 3–8** three more times to complete all four petals.

Fasten off and weave in all ends. Attach one poppy on top of another to make each of the three flowers.

POPPY IN WITH A GOOD PROJECT...

Crochet a remembrance poppy brooch by making the Poppy and Center only. Then simply attach a safety pin to the back of the flower.

CENTER (MAKE 3)

Rnd 1: with **2.5mm** hook and **yellow DK** yarn, sc 10 in magic ring [10]

Rnd 2: change to **black DK** yarn, (sl st + ch 3 + sl st + ch 3 in next st, sl st + ch 3) 5 times, sl st in next st

Fasten off and weave in all ends. Attach to the center of the poppy flower.

STEM (MAKE 3)

Rnd 1: turn poppy over and join **green DK** yarn in any back loop from **Row 3** of the poppy. With a **2.5mm** hook, working in BLO, sc in each st around [16]

Rnd 2: (sc2tog, sc 2) 4 times [12]

Rnd 3: (sc2tog, sc 2) 3 times [9]

Rnd 4: sc in each st around [9]

Begin to stuff with fiberfill.

Rnd 5: (sc2tog, sc 1) 3 times [6]

Rnds 6–14: sc in each st around [6]

Sl st in next st, finish stuffing with fiberfill, insert floral wire into stem leaving 2.5cm (1in) of wire extending past the stem. Fasten off and weave in ends. Bend the head of the poppy slightly forward (1).

LEAF (MAKE 3)

Rnd 1: with **2.5mm** hook and **green DK** yarn, ch 10, sc in 2nd ch from hook, sc 8, ch 2, working on the other side of the foundation ch, sc 1, (ch 4, sc in 2nd ch from hook, sc in next 2 ch sts, sc 2) 4 times [32]

Rnd 2: (ch 4, sc in 2nd ch from hook, sc in next 2 ch sts, sc 2) 5 times, working last sc in ch-2 space [25]

Fasten off and weave in all ends.

Attach a leaf to each stem (2).

Insert poppies in vase.

Leaf Chart

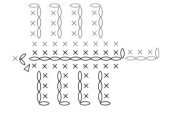

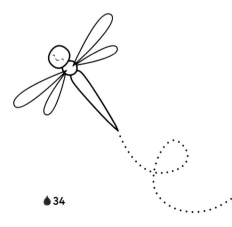

STRAWBERRY PLANT

Materials

- 3.5mm (E/4) and 2.5mm (C/2) crochet hooks
- Paintbox Yarns Cotton Aran yarn: one 50g (1¾oz) ball each of Pillar Red (**red**), Champagne White (**cream**), and Soft Fudge (**brown**)
- Paintbox Yarns Cotton DK yarn: one 50g (1¾oz) ball each of Spearmint Green (**green**), Pillar Red (**red**), Daffodil Yellow (**yellow**), and Paper White (**white**)
- Scraps of **black** and **pink** yarn
- 8mm safety eyes
- Fiberfill stuffing
- 26- and 20-gauge floral wire
- Yarn needle
- Stitch marker

Finished size

18cm (7in) tall by 12.5cm (5in) wide

Gauge

5 sc sts and 6 rows = 2.5cm (1in) using Aran yarn

6 sc sts and 7 rows = 2.5cm (1in) using DK yarn

POT

Rnd 1: with **3.5mm** hook and **red Aran** yarn, sc 6 in magic ring [6]

Rnd 2: 2 sc in each st around [12]

Rnd 3: (sc 1, 2 sc in next st) 6 times [18]

Rnd 4: (sc 2, 2 sc in next st) 6 times [24]

Rnd 5: (sc 3, 2 sc in next st) 6 times [30]

Rnd 6: (sc 4, 2 sc in next st) 6 times [36]

Rnd 7: (sc 5, 2 sc in next st) 6 times [42]

Rnd 8: working in BLO, sc in each st around [42]

Rnds 9–13: sc in each st around [42]

Rnd 14: (sc 6, 2 sc in next st) 6 times [48]

Rnd 15: sc in each st around [48]

Rnd 16: change to **cream Aran** yarn, sc in each st around [48]

Rnd 17: sc in each st around [48]

Place 8mm safety eyes between **Rnds 13 and 14**, with 5 sts in between. Begin to stuff with fiberfill. Do not finish off and cut yarn. Make the dirt before moving on to **Rnd 18**.

Rnd 18: place the dirt in the pot and line up the stitches from **Rnd 17** of the pot and **Rnd 8** of

the dirt. With the yarn used to make the pot, sc in each st around, working in both loops of both pieces to join them together (see Making Up: Crocheting Two Pieces Together) [48]

Rnd 19: ch 1, sc in each st around, join with sl st in first st [48]

Rnd 20: sl st in each st around [48]

Invisible fasten off (see Finishing: Invisible Fasten Off) and weave in ends. Add stitches for the mouth and cheeks using **black** and **pink** yarn (see Making Up: Stitching Facial Details).

Begin shaping by inserting needle from center bottom to center top, then take needle back down from center top to slightly off center bottom and back up to center top. Pull to create an indentation in the bottom of the pot. Fasten off and weave in ends.

DIRT

Rnd 1: with **3.5mm** hook and **brown Aran** yarn, sc 6 in magic ring [6]

Rnd 2: 2 sc in each st around [12]

Rnd 3: (sc 1, 2 sc in next st) 6 times [18]

Rnd 4: (sc 2, 2 sc in next st) 6 times [24]

Rnd 5: (sc 3, 2 sc in next st) 6 times [30]

Rnd 6: (sc 4, 2 sc in next st) 6 times [36]

Rnd 7: (sc 5, 2 sc in next st) 6 times [42]

Rnd 8: (sc 6, 2 sc in next st) 6 times [48]

Invisible fasten off and weave in ends.

LEAF (MAKE 12)

Rnd 1: cut a 10cm (4in) piece of 26-gauge floral wire. With **2.5mm** hook and **green DK** yarn, ch 8, hold wire behind the foundation ch and crochet the following sts around the wire (see Making Up: Crocheting with Floral Wire): sc in 2nd ch from hook, hdc 1, dc 1, 2 tr in next st, dc 1, hdc 1, sc 1 (1), ch 2, bend wire end behind sts, working on the other side of the foundation ch, sc 1, hdc 1, dc 1, 2 tr in next st, dc 1, hdc 1, sc 1 (2) [18]

Rnd 2: (sc in next st, ch-2 picot) 18 times, sl st in next st, ch 5 (3), hold floral wire end behind ch 5 and crochet the following sts around the wire, sc in 2nd ch from hook, sc 3 (4) [39]

Fasten off and weave in ends. Bunch three leaves together and twist wires together (5).

Insert the leaves into the pot.

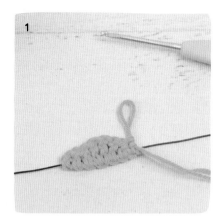

Leaf Chart

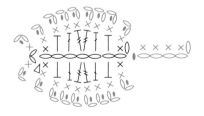

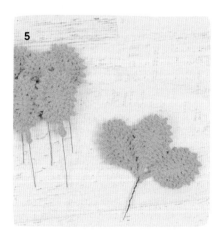

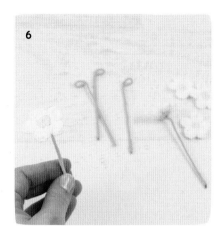

BLOSSOM (MAKE 5)

Rnd 1: with **2.5mm** hook and **yellow DK** yarn, sc 5 in magic ring [5]

Rnd 2: change to **white DK** yarn, (sl st + ch 2 + 2 dc + ch 2 + sl st in next st) 5 times, sl st in next st [5 petals]

Fasten off and weave in ends. Make five yarn-wrapped wire stems (6) (see Making Up: Yarn-Wrapped Stems). Attach blossom to yarn-wrapped wire stems. Insert stems in pot.

STRAWBERRY (MAKE 5)

Rnd 1: with **2.5mm** hook and **red DK** yarn, sc 6 in magic ring [6]

Rnd 2: (sc 1, 2 sc in next st) 3 times [9]

Rnd 3: (sc 2, 2 sc in next st) 3 times [12]

Rnd 4: (sc 3, 2 sc in next st) 3 times [15]

Rnd 5: (sc 4, 2 sc in next st) 3 times [18]

Rnd 6: sc in each st around [18]

Rnd 7: (sc2tog, sc 1) 6 times [12]

Rnd 8: (sc2tog) 6 times [6]

Fasten off and weave in ends.

STRAWBERRY STEM (MAKE 5)

Rnd 1: with **2.5mm** hook and **green DK** yarn, ch 4, sl st in first ch to form a circle, (ch 6 + sl st in circle) 5 times

Fasten off and attach to the top of the strawberry. Make five yarn-wrapped wire stems (7) (see Making Up: Yarn-Wrapped Stems). Insert the wire stems into the tops of the strawberries.

Insert the stems in the pot.

Believe it or not, the color orange is named
after the citrus fruit. Legend has it that, prior
to the 17th century, carrots were only white
and purple until Dutch growers cultivated an
orange variety as a tribute to William of Orange.

GERBERA

Materials

- 3.5mm (E/4) and 2.5mm (C/2) crochet hooks
- Paintbox Yarns Cotton Aran yarn: one 50g (1¾oz) ball each of Champagne White (**cream**) and Washed Teal (**blue**)
- Paintbox Yarns Cotton DK yarn: one 50g (1¾oz) ball each of Pure Black (**black**), Blood Orange (**dark orange**), Mandarin Orange (**orange**), and Grass Green (**green**)
- Scraps of **black** and **pink** yarn
- 7mm safety eyes
- Fiberfill stuffing
- Chenille stem (pipe cleaner)
- Yarn needle
- Stitch marker

Finished size

18cm (7in) tall by 7.5cm (3in) wide

Gauge

5 sc sts and 6 rows = 2.5cm (1in) using Aran yarn

6 sc sts and 7 rows = 2.5cm (1in) using DK yarn

BUD VASE

Rnd 1: with **3.5mm** hook and **cream Aran** yarn, sc 6 in magic ring [6]

Rnd 2: 2 sc in each st around [12]

Rnd 3: (sc 1, 2 sc in next st) 6 times [18]

Rnd 4: (sc 2, 2 sc in next st) 6 times [24]

Rnd 5: (sc 3, 2 sc in next st) 6 times [30]

Rnd 6: working in BLO, sc in each st around [30]

Rnd 7: (sc 4, 2 sc in next st) 6 times [36]

Rnds 8–9: sc in each st around [36]

Rnd 10: (sc 5, 2 sc in next st) 6 times [42]

Rnds 11–13: sc in each st around [42]

Rnd 14: (sc2tog, sc 5) 6 times [36]

Rnd 15: (sc2tog, sc 4) 6 times [30]

Rnd 16: (sc2tog, sc 3) 6 times [24]

Rnd 17: (sc2tog, sc 6) 3 times [21]

Place 7mm safety eyes between **Rnds 11 and 12**, with 4 sts in between. Stuff with fiberfill. Do not finish off and cut yarn. Make the water before moving on to **Rnd 18**.

Rnd 18: place the water in the vase and line up the stitches from **Rnd 17** of the vase and **Rnd 4** of the water. With the yarn used to make the vase, sc in each st around, working in both loops of both pieces to join them together (see Making Up: Crocheting Two Pieces Together) [21]

Rnds 19–29: sc in each st around [21]

Rnd 30: sl st in each st around [21]

Invisible fasten off (see Finishing: Invisible Fasten Off) and weave in ends. Add stitches for the mouth and cheeks using **black** and **pink** yarn (see Making Up: Stitching Facial Details). Begin shaping by inserting needle from center bottom to center top, then take needle back down from center top to slightly off center bottom and back up to center top. Pull to create an indentation in the bottom of the vase. Fasten off and weave in ends.

WATER

Rnd 1: with **3.5mm** hook and **blue Aran** yarn, sc 6 in magic ring [6]

Rnd 2: 2 sc in each st around [12]

Rnd 3: (sc 1, 2 sc in next st) 6 times [18]

Rnd 4: (sc 5, 2 sc in next st) 3 times [21]

Invisible fasten off and weave in ends.

FLOWER

Rnd 1: with **2.5mm** hook and **black DK** yarn, sc 6 in magic ring [6]

Rnd 2: 2 sc in each st around [12]

Rnd 3: (sc 1, 2 sc in next st) 6 times [18]

Rnd 4: change to **dark orange DK** yarn, working in BLO, (sc 2, 2 sc in next st) 6 times [24]

Rnd 5: change to **orange DK** yarn, (sl st in FLO of next st, ch 12, dc in 4th ch from hook, dc in next 8 ch sts, sl st in FLO of next unworked st from **Rnd 5**) 12 times [12 petals]

Rnd 6: sl st around each flower petal

Fasten off and weave in ends.

Rnd 7: join **dark orange** yarn in a **black** front loop from **Rnd 3**, working in FLO (sc in next st, ch 2) 18 times (1) [54]

Fasten off and weave in ends.

Rnd 8: turn flower over, join **green DK** yarn in a **dark orange** back loop from **Rnd 6**, working in BLO, sc in each st around (2) [24]

Rnd 9: (sc2tog, sc 2) 6 times [18]

Rnd 10: (sc2tog, sc 1) 6 times [12]

Rnd 11: sc in each st around [12]

Stuff the stem with fiberfill stuffing up to this rnd.

Rnd 12: (sc2tog) 6 times [6]

Rnds 13–27: sc in each st around [6]

Sl st in next st, insert chenille stem into stem leaving 2.5cm (1in) extending past the stem (3). Fasten off and weave in ends. Insert gerbera in bud vase.

MARIGOLD

Materials

- 3.5mm (E/4) and 2.5mm (C/2) crochet hooks
- Paintbox Yarns Cotton Aran yarn: one 50g (1¾oz) ball each of Vanilla Cream (**cream**) and Soft Fudge (**brown**)
- Paintbox Yarns Cotton DK yarn: one 50g (1¾oz) ball each of Mandarin Orange (**orange**) and Grass Green (**green**)
- Scraps of **black** and **pink** yarn
- 7mm safety eyes
- Fiberfill stuffing
- 20-gauge floral wire
- Yarn needle
- Stitch marker

Finished size

14cm (5½in) tall by 7.5cm (3in) wide

Gauge

5 sc sts and 6 rows = 2.5cm (1in) using Aran yarn

6 sc sts and 7 rows = 2.5cm (1in) using DK yarn

DIRT

Rnd 1: with a 3.5mm hook and **brown Aran** yarn, sc 6 in magic ring [6]

Rnd 2: 2 sc in each st around [12]

Rnd 3: (sc 1, 2 sc in next st) 6 times [18]

Rnd 4: (sc 2, 2 sc in next st) 6 times [24]

Rnd 5: (sc 3, 2 sc in next st) 6 times [30]

Rnd 6: (sc 4, 2 sc in next st) 6 times [36]

Rnd 7: (sc 5, 2 sc in next st) 6 times [42]

Invisible fasten off (see Finishing: Invisible Fasten Off) and weave in ends.

POT

Rnd 1: with a 3.5mm hook and **cream Aran** yarn, sc 6 in magic ring [6]

Rnd 2: 2 sc in each st around [12]

Rnd 3: (sc 1, 2 sc in next st) 6 times [18]

Rnd 4: (sc 2, 2 sc in next st) 6 times [24]

Rnd 5: (sc 3, 2 sc in next st) 6 times [30]

Rnd 6: (sc 4, 2 sc in next st) 6 times [36]

Rnd 7: working in BLO, sc in each st around [36]

Rnds 8–11: sc in each st around [36]

Rnd 12: (sc 5, 2 sc in next st) 6 times [42]

Rnds 13–15: sc in each st around [42]

Place 7mm safety eyes between **Rnds 11 and 12**, with 4 sts in between. Begin to stuff with fiberfill. Do not fasten off and cut yarn.

Rnd 16: place dirt in pot, lining up stitches from **Rnd 15** of pot and **Rnd 7** of dirt. With **cream Aran** yarn, sc in each st around working in both loops of both pieces to join them together [42]

Rnd 17: ch 1, sc in each st around, join with sl st in first st [42]

Rnd 18: sl st in each st around [42]

Invisible fasten off and weave in ends. Stitch on mouth and cheeks using **black** and **pink** yarn (see Making Up: Stitching Facial Details). Begin shaping by inserting needle from center bottom to center top, then insert needle back down from center top to slightly off center bottom. Insert needle from center bottom to center top. Pull to create indentation in bottom of pot. Fasten off and weave in ends.

MARIGOLD (MAKE 3)

Rnd 1: with a 2.5mm hook and **orange DK** yarn, sc 10 in magic ring [10]

Rnd 2: working in FLO, (ch 4, skip next st, sc 1) 5 times [5 ch-4 spaces]

Rnd 3: (ch 5, 1 sc in next sc st) 5 times [5 ch-5 spaces]

Rnd 4: working in ch-5 spaces from **Rnd 3**, (sc in next ch-5 space + *ch 4 + dc in 4th ch from hook + sc 1, repeat from * 3 times) 5 times [15 petals]

Rnd 5: working in ch-4 spaces from **Rnd 2**, (sc in next ch-4 space + *ch 4 + dc in 4th ch from hook + sc 1, repeat from * 2 times) 5 times [10 petals]

Fasten off and weave in ends. Turn flower over.

Rnd 6: join **green DK** yarn in a back loop from **Rnd 2**, sc in each back loop around (1) [10]

Rnd 7: (sc 3, sc2tog) twice [8]

Rnd 8: (sc 2, sc2tog) twice [6]

Rnds 9-18: sc in each st around [6]

Fasten off. Stuff stem with fiberfill and insert floral wire leaving the wire 2.5cm (1in) longer than stem. With yarn needle weave through FLO to close opening. Weave in ends. Make a total of three flowers. Crochet second and third flowers to **Rnd 14** only.

CENTER (MAKE 3)

Rnd 1: with a 2.5mm hook and **orange DK** yarn, sc 5 in magic ring [5]

Rnd 2: (sl st + ch 4 + dc in 4th ch from hook + sl st + ch 4 + dc in 4th ch from hook + sl st) 5 times [10 petals]

Fasten off and attach to center of flower.

LEAF (MAKE 6)

Rnd 1: with a 2.5mm hook and **green DK** yarn, ch 12, sc in 2nd ch from hook, sc 9, 3 sc in last ch, turn to work on the other side of the foundation ch, sc 9, 2 sc in last st [24]

Rnds 2–6 are not complete rnds.

Rnd 2: sc in next 9 sts, turn [9]

Rnd 3: ch 1, sc in next 9 sts, 3 sc in next st, sc in next 9 sts, turn [21]

Rnd 4: ch 1, sc in next 10 sts, 2 sc in next 2 sts, sc in next 7 sts, turn [21]

Rnd 5: ch 1, sc in next 8 sts, 2 sc in next 2 sts, sc in next 9 sts, turn [21]

Rnd 6: ch 1, sc in next 10 sts, sl st in next st [11]

Fasten off and weave in ends. Make a total of six leaves and attach two leaves to bottom of each stem (2). Insert all three flowers into dirt after attaching leaves to stems.

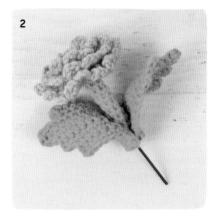

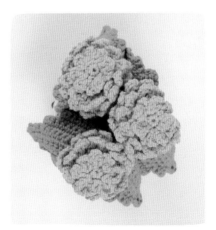

PRICKLY PEAR CACTUS

POT

Rnd 1: with **orange** yarn, sc 6 in magic ring [6]

Rnd 2: 2 sc in each st around [12]

Rnd 3: (sc 1, 2 sc in next st) 6 times [18]

Rnd 4: (sc 2, 2 sc in next st) 6 times [24]

Rnd 5: (sc 3, 2 sc in next st) 6 times [30]

Rnd 6: (sc 4, 2 sc in next st) 6 times [36]

Rnd 7: working in BLO, sc in each st around [36]

Rnds 8–11: sc in each st around [36]

Rnd 12: (sc 5, 2 sc in next st) 6 times [42]

Rnds 13–15: sc in each st around [42]

Place 7mm safety eyes between **Rnds 11 and 12**, with 4 sts in between. Begin to stuff with fiberfill. Do not finish off and cut yarn. Make the dirt before moving on to **Rnd 16**.

Rnd 16: place the dirt in the pot and line up the stitches from **Rnd 15** of the pot and **Rnd 7** of the dirt. With the yarn used to make the pot, sc in each st around, working in both loops of both pieces to join them together (see Making Up: Crocheting Two Pieces Together) [42]

Rnd 17: ch 1, sc in each st around, join with sl st in first st [42]

Rnd 18: sl st in each st around [42]

Invisible fasten off (see Finishing: Invisible Fasten Off) and weave in ends. Add stitches for the mouth and cheeks using **black** and **pink** yarn (see Making Up: Stitching Facial Details).

Begin shaping by inserting needle from center bottom to center top, then take needle back down from center top to slightly off center bottom and back up to center top. Pull to create an indentation in the bottom of the pot. Fasten off and weave in ends.

DIRT

Rnd 1: with **brown** yarn, sc 6 in magic ring [6]

Rnd 2: 2 sc in each st around [12]

Rnd 3: (sc 1, 2 sc in next st) 6 times [18]

Rnd 4: (sc 2, 2 sc in next st) 6 times [24]

Rnd 5: (sc 3, 2 sc in next st) 6 times [30]

Rnd 6: (sc 4, 2 sc in next st) 6 times [36]

Rnd 7: (sc 5, 2 sc in next st) 6 times [42]

Invisible fasten off and weave in ends.

CACTUS PART A

Rnd 1: with **green** yarn, sc 6 in magic ring [6]

Rnd 2: 2 sc in each st around [12]

Rnd 3: (sc 1, 2 sc in next st) 6 times [18]

Rnd 4: (sc 2, 2 sc in next st) 6 times [24]

Rnds 5–10: sc in each st around [24]

Rnd 11: (sc2tog, sc 2) 6 times [18]

Rnd 12: sc in each st around [18]

Rnd 13: (sc2tog, sc 1) 6 times [12]

Rnd 14: sc in each st around [12]

Fasten off, leaving a long yarn tail. Stuff lightly with fiberfill and flatten. With yarn needle and yarn tail, sew **Rnd 14** of Part A to the dirt.

CACTUS PART B

Rnd 1: with **green** yarn, sc 6 in magic ring [6]

Rnd 2: 2 sc in each st around [12]

Rnd 3: (sc 1, 2 sc in next st) 6 times [18]

Rnds 4–7: sc in each st around [18]

Rnd 8: (sc2tog, sc 1) 6 times [12]

Rnds 9–10: sc in each st around [12]

Fasten off, leaving a long yarn tail. Stuff lightly with fiberfill and flatten. With yarn needle and yarn tail, sew Part B to the top of Part A at an angle.

CACTUS PART C

Rnd 1: with **green** yarn, sc 6 in magic ring [6]

Rnd 2: 2 sc in each st around [12]

Rnds 3–5: sc in each st around [12]

Rnd 6: (sc2tog) 6 times [6]

Rnd 7: sc in each st around [6]

Fasten off, leaving a long yarn tail. Stuff lightly with fiberfill and flatten. With yarn needle and yarn tail, sew **Rnd 7** of Part C to the dirt.

YOU PRICKLE MY FANCY...

Make and give one as a gift for someone who is not feeling well. Just add a tag that says, "I hope thistle make you feel a little better!"

FLOWER (MAKE 3)

Rnd 1: with **dark orange** yarn, sc 5 in magic ring [5]

Rnd 2: (sl st + ch 2 + dc 1 + ch 2 + sl st) 5 times [5 petals]

Fasten off and weave in ends. Attach a flower to the top of each piece of cactus.

SEED PACKETS

Materials

- 3.5mm (E/4) and 2.5mm (C/2) crochet hooks
- Paintbox Yarns Cotton Aran yarn: one 50g (1¾oz) ball of Champagne White (**cream**)
- Paintbox Yarns Cotton DK yarn: one 50g (1¾oz) ball each of Mandarin Orange (**orange**), Spearmint Green (**green**), Blood Orange (**dark orange**), and Coffee Bean (**brown**)
- Scraps of **black** yarn
- 5mm and 6mm safety eyes
- Fiberfill stuffing
- Yarn needle
- Stitch marker

Finished size

10cm (4in) tall by 7.5cm (3in) wide

Gauge

5 sc sts and 6 rows = 2.5cm (1in) using Aran yarn

6 sc sts and 7 rows = 2.5cm (1in) using DK yarn

PACKET (MAKE 2)

Rnd 1: with **3.5mm** hook and **cream Aran** yarn, ch 15, sc in 2nd ch from hook, sc 12, 3 sc in last st, working on the other side of the foundation ch, sc in next 12 sts, 2 sc in last st [30]

Rnds 2–21: sc in each st around [30]

Row 22: sc 2, should now be in the top left corner of the packet, ch 1, turn, working in BLO, sc2tog, sc 11, sc2tog, turn [13]

Row 23: ch 1, sc in each st across, turn [13]

Row 24: ch 1, sc2tog, sc 9, sc2tog, turn [11]

Row 25: ch 1, sc in each st across [11]

Fasten off and weave in ends. Add the word "seeds" in black yarn on the front of the packet.

CARROT APPLIQUÉ

Rnd 1: with **2.5mm** hook and **orange DK** yarn, ch 12, 2 dc in 4th ch from hook (first three skipped chs count as dc), dc 1, hdc 3, sc 3, sc + ch 3 + sc in last st, working on the other side of the foundation ch, sc 3, hdc 3, dc 1, 4 dc in last st, join rnd with sl st in first dc st [26]

Rnd 2: ch 1, 2 sc in next 2 sts, sc 8, sc + ch 1 + dc + ch 1 + sc in ch-3 space, sc 8, 2 sc in next 3 sts, join rnd with sl st in first sc [31]

Rnd 3: join **green DK** yarn to top of carrot, (ch 10, sc in 2nd ch from hook, sc 7, sl st 1, sl st in same st as where you joined green yarn) 3 times [30]

Fasten off and weave in ends. Attach carrot to the front of the packet. Place 5mm safety eyes through both the carrot and the packet between **Rnds 1 and 2**, using the photo as a guide. Add stitches for the mouth using **black** yarn (see Making Up: Stitching Facial Details).

Place a small amount of fiberfill behind the safety eyes. Secure packet flap to back of packet.

PUMPKIN APPLIQUÉ

Rnd 1: with **2.5mm** hook and **dark orange DK** yarn, sc 6 in magic ring [6]

Rnd 2: 2 sc in each st around [12]

Rnd 3: hdc 1, 2 hdc in next st, (sc 1, 2 sc in next st) 3 times, hdc 1, 2 hdc in next st, sc 1, 2 sc in last st [18]

Rnd 4: hdc 1, 2 hdc in next st, 2 dc in next st, dc 1, 2 dc in next st, hdc 6, 2 dc in next st, dc 1, 2 dc in next st, 2 hdc in next st, hdc 1, sc 2 [24]

Rnd 5: sc 2, 2 sc in next st, hdc 1, 2 hdc in next st, hdc 3, 2 hdc in next st, sc 2, 2 hdc in next 2 sts, sc 2, 2 hdc in next st, hdc 3, 2 hdc in next st, hdc 1, 2 sc in next st, sc 2 [32]

Rnd 6: sl st 2, sc 1, 2 sc in next st, (sc 3, 2 sc in next st) 2 times, sl st 2, 2 sc in next st, sc 2, 2 sc in next st, sl st 2, 2 sc in next st, (sc 3, sl st 2) 2 times, sc 1, sl st 2, [40]

Rnd 7: join **brown DK** yarn to top center of pumpkin, ch 6, hdc in 2nd ch from hook, sc 4, sl st in next st of pumpkin

Fasten off and weave in ends. Attach pumpkin to the front of the packet. Place 6mm safety eyes through both the pumpkin and the packet between **Rnds 3 and 4,** using the photo as a guide. Add stitches for the mouth using **black** yarn (see Making Up: Stitching Facial Details).

Place a small amount of fiberfill behind the safety eyes. Secure packet flap to back of packet.

LEAF

Rnd 1: with **2.5mm** hook and **green DK** yarn, ch 7, sl st in 2nd ch from hook, sc 1, hdc 1, dc 1, hdc 1, 3 sc in last st, working on the other side of the foundation ch, hdc 1, dc 1, hdc 1, sc 1, sl st 1, sl st in beginning skipped ch st

Invisible fasten off and weave in ends. Attach to the pumpkin next to the stem.

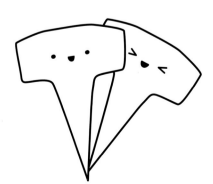

SEED A GiFT?

Do not seal the envelope closed; instead insert a gift card and a note that says "Wishing you a seed-cessful recovery!", "Hope to seed you soon!", or "We are rooting for you!"

SNAIL

Materials

- 2.5mm (C/2) crochet hook
- Paintbox Yarns Cotton DK yarn: one 50g (1¾oz) ball each of Peach Orange (**peach**) and Mandarin Orange (**orange**)
- 7mm safety eyes
- Fiberfill stuffing
- Yarn needle
- Stitch marker

Finished size

7.5cm (3in) tall by 9cm (3 ½in) wide

Gauge

6 sc sts and 7 rows = 2.5cm (1in)

ANTENNA (MAKE 2)

Rnd 1: with **peach** yarn, ch 7, working in back bump loops, sc in 2nd ch from hook, sl st in next 5 ch sts [6]

Fasten off and do not weave in ends.

BODY

Rnd 1: with **peach** yarn, sc 6 in magic ring [6]

Rnd 2: 2 sc in each st around [12]

Rnd 3: (sc 1, 2 sc in next st) 6 times [18]

Rnd 4: (sc 2, 2 sc in next st) 6 times [24]

Rnds 5–8: sc in each st around [24]

Rnd 9: (sc2tog, sc 2) 6 times [18]

Rnd 10: sc in each st around [18]

Place 7mm safety eyes between **Rnds 5 and 6**, with 8 sts in between. Attach antennae between **Rnds 2 and 3**, directly above the eyes. Begin to stuff with fiberfill.

Rnd 11: (sc2tog, sc 4) 3 times [15]

Rnd 12: sc in each st around [15]

Rnd 13: (sc2tog, sc 3) 3 times [12]

Finish stuffing head with fiberfill. Do not stuff the rest of the body.

Rnds 14–29: sc in each st around [12]

Rnd 30: (sc2tog, sc 2) 3 times [9]

Rnd 31: sc in each st around [9]

Rnd 32: (sc2tog, sc 1) 3 times [6]

Fasten off, leaving a long yarn tail. With a yarn needle, weave the tail through FLO to close the opening. Weave in ends.

SHELL

Rnd 1: with **orange** yarn, sc 7 in magic ring [7]

Work in back bump loops only for **Rnds 2–6**.

Rnd 2: 2 sc in each st around [14]

Rnd 3: (hdc 1, 2 hdc in next st) 7 times [21]

Rnd 4: (hdc 2, 2 hdc in next st) 7 times [28]

Rnd 5: (hdc 3, 2 hdc in next st) 7 times [35]

Rnd 6: hdc in each st around [35]

Sc in next st, sl st in next st.

End with sc in next st, sl st in next st to end spiral.

Fasten off and weave in ends. Repeat **Rnds 1–6** for the second half of the shell, leaving a 60cm (24in) yarn tail. Place the shell pieces with right sides facing out. With a yarn tail and yarn needle, whip stitch together through BLO of both pieces (1).

Stuff lightly with fiberfill as you sew the two halves together. Attach the shell to the body.

YOU SNAILED IT...

Did you know it takes over 33 hours for a snail to travel a mile? That they have the most teeth of any animal? Or that they can sleep for three years?

1

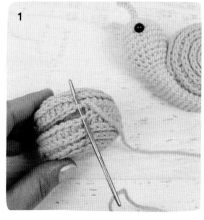

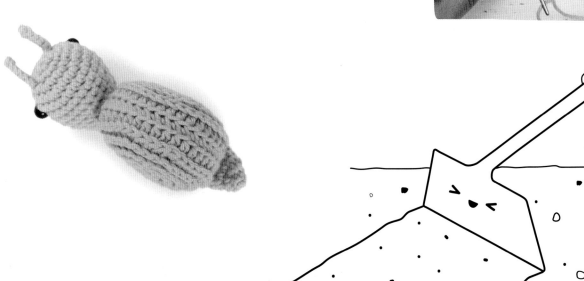

Bright colors attract the eye and yellow is the top attention-getter because it's the most luminous of all the colors of the spectrum. The color of the sun is actually white but, due to the scattering of light, the color we see becomes yellow.

BILLY BUTTONS

Materials

- 3.5mm (E/4) and 2.5mm (C/2) crochet hooks
- Paintbox Yarns Cotton Aran yarn: one 50g (1¾oz) ball each of Champagne White (**cream**) and Washed Teal (**blue**)
- Paintbox Yarns Cotton DK yarn: one 50g (1¾oz) ball each of Buttercup Yellow (**yellow**) and Grass Green (**green**)
- Scraps of **black** and **pink** yarn
- 7mm safety eyes
- Fiberfill stuffing
- 20-gauge floral wire
- Yarn needle
- Stitch marker

Finished size

20cm (8in) tall by 7.5cm (3in) wide

Gauge

5 sc sts and 6 rows = 2.5cm (1in) using Aran yarn

6 sc sts and 7 rows = 2.5cm (1in) using DK yarn

VASE

Rnd 1: with **3.5mm** hook and **cream Aran** yarn, sc 6 in magic ring [6]

Rnd 2: 2 sc in each st around [12]

Rnd 3: (sc 1, 2 sc in next st) 6 times [18]

Rnd 4: (sc 2, 2 sc in next st) 6 times [24]

Rnd 5: (sc 3, 2 sc in next st) 6 times [30]

Rnd 6: (sc 4, 2 sc in next st) 6 times [36]

Rnd 7: working in BLO, sc in each st around [36]

Rnd 8: sc in each st around [36]

Rnd 9: (sc 5, 2 sc in next st) 6 times [42]

Rnds 10–16: sc in each st around [42]

Rnd 17: (sc2tog, sc 5) 6 times [36]

Rnd 18: (sc 2, sc2tog, sc 2) 6 times [30]

Rnd 19: (sc2tog, sc 3) 6 times [24]

Place 7mm safety eyes between **Rnds 11 and 12**, with 4 sts in between. Stuff with fiberfill. Do not finish off and cut yarn. Make the water before moving on to **Rnd 20**.

Rnd 20: place the water in the vase and line up the stitches from **Rnd 19** of the vase and **Rnd 4** of the water. With the yarn used to make the vase, sc in each st around, working in both loops of both pieces to join them together (see Making Up: Crocheting Two Pieces Together) [24]

Rnds 21–22: sc in each st around [24]

Rnd 23: (sc 3, 2 sc in next st) 6 times [30]

Rnds 24–25: sc in each st around [30]

Rnd 26: sl st in each st around [30]

Invisible fasten off (see Finishing: Invisible Fasten Off) and weave in ends. Add stitches for the mouth and cheeks using **black** and **pink** yarn (see Making Up: Stitching Facial Details). Begin shaping by inserting needle from center bottom to center top, then take needle back down from center top to slightly off center bottom and back up to center top. Pull to create an indentation in the bottom of the vase. Fasten off and weave in ends.

WATER

Rnd 1: with **3.5mm** hook and **blue Aran** yarn sc 6 in magic ring [6]

Rnd 2: 2 sc in each st around [12]

Rnd 3: (sc 1, 2 sc in next st) 6 times [18]

Rnd 4: (sc 2, 2 sc in next st) 6 times [24]

Invisible fasten off and weave in ends.

FLOWER HEAD (MAKE 7)

Rnd 1: with **2.5mm** hook and **yellow DK** yarn, sc 6 in magic ring [6]

Rnd 2: 2 sc in each st around [12]

Rnd 3: (sc 1, 2 sc in next st) 6 times [18]

Rnd 4: (sc 1, 3 sc in next st) 6 times [24]

Rnds 5–6: sc in each st around [24]

Begin to stuff with fiberfill.

Rnd 7: (sc2tog, sc 2) 6 times [18]

Rnd 8: sc in each st around [18]

Rnd 9: (sc2tog, sc 1) 6 times [12]

Rnd 10: (sc2tog) 6 times [6]

Finish stuffing.

Invisible fasten off, leaving a long yarn tail. With a yarn needle, weave the tail through FLO to close the opening. Weave in ends.

YARN-WRAPPED STEM (MAKE 7)

Cut a 10-cm (4-in) length of floral wire and place a drop of hot glue on one end. Wrap **green DK** yarn around the entire length of the wire, then place another drop of hot glue at the end (1). Insert the stems into the flower heads.

Insert the billy buttons into the vase (2).

CALLA LiLY

Materials

- 3.5mm (E/4) and 2.5mm (C/2) crochet hooks
- Paintbox Yarns Cotton Aran yarn: one 50g (1¾oz) ball each of Daffodil Yellow (**yellow**) and Washed Teal (**blue**)
- Paintbox Yarns Cotton DK yarn: one 50g (1¾oz) ball each of Paper White (**white**), Buttercup Yellow (**dark yellow**), and Lime Green (**lime green**)
- Scraps of **pink** and **black** yarn
- 7mm safety eyes
- Fiberfill stuffing
- Chenille stem (pipe cleaner)
- Yarn needle
- Stitch marker

Finished size

18cm (7in) tall by 7.5cm (3in) wide

Gauge

5 sc sts and 6 rows = 2.5cm (1in) using Aran yarn

6 sc sts and 7 rows = 2.5cm (1in) using DK yarn

VASE

Rnd 1: with **3.5mm** hook and **yellow Aran** yarn, sc 6 in magic ring [6]

Rnd 2: 2 sc in each st around [12]

Rnd 3: (sc 1, 2 sc in next st) 6 times [18]

Rnd 4: (sc 2, 2 sc in next st) 6 times [24]

Rnd 5: (sc 3, 2 sc in next st) 6 times [30]

Rnd 6: (sc 4, 2 sc in next st) 6 times [36]

Rnd 7: working in BLO, sc in each st around [36]

Rnd 8: sc in each st around [36]

Rnd 9: (sc 5, 2 sc in next st) 6 times [42]

Rnds 10–16: sc in each st around [42]

Rnd 17: (sc2tog, sc 5) 6 times [36]

Rnd 18: (sc 2, sc2tog, sc 2) 6 times [30]

Rnd 19: (sc2tog, sc 3) 6 times [24]

Place 7mm safety eyes between **Rnds 11 and 12**, with 4 sts in between. Stuff with fiberfill. Do not finish off and cut yarn. Make the water before moving on to **Rnd 20**.

Rnd 20: place the water in the vase and line up the stitches from **Rnd 19** of the vase and **Rnd 4** of the water. With the yarn used to make the vase, sc in each st around working in both loops of both pieces to join them together (see Making Up: Crocheting Two Pieces Together) [24]

Rnds 21–22: sc in each st around [24]

Rnd 23: (sc 3, 2 sc in next st) repeat 6 times [30]

Rnds 24–25: sc in each st around [30]

Rnd 26: sl st in each st around [30]

Invisible fasten off (see Finishing: Invisible Fasten Off) and weave in ends. Add stitches for the mouth and cheeks using **black** and **pink** yarn (see Making Up: Stitching Facial Details). Begin shaping by inserting needle from center bottom to center top, then take needle back down from center top to slightly off center bottom and back up to center top. Pull to create an indentation in the bottom of the vase. Fasten off and weave in ends.

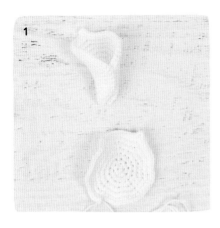

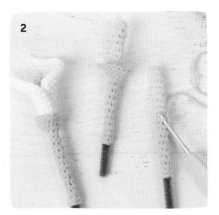

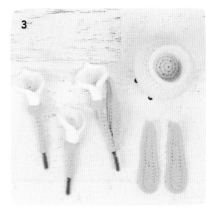

WATER

Rnd 1: with **3.5mm** hook and **blue Aran** yarn, sc 6 in magic ring [6]

Rnd 2: 2 sc in each st around [12]

Rnd 3: (sc 1, 2 sc in next st) 6 times [18]

Rnd 4: (sc 2, 2 sc in next st) 6 times [24]

Invisible fasten off and weave in ends.

CALLA LILY (MAKE 3)

Rnd 1: with **2.5mm** hook and **white DK** yarn, sc 5 in magic ring [5]

Rnd 2: 2 sc in each st around [10]

Rnd 3: 2 sc in each st around [20]

Rnd 4: (sc 1, 2 sc in next st) 10 times [30]

Rnd 5: (sc 2, 2 sc in next st) 10 times [40]

Rnd 6: (sc 3, 2 sc in next st) 10 times [50]

Rnd 7: (sc 4, 2 sc in next st) repeat 4 times, sc 4, sc + ch 3 + sc in next st, (sc 4, 2 sc in next st) 5 times [60]

Invisible fasten off, leaving a long tail. Form the lily into a funnel with the yarn tail at the

bottom and the ch-3 from **Rnd 7** centered at the top. Sew 2.5cm (1in) of the lily together, leaving a hole at the bottom for the stem (1).

STEM (MAKE 3)

Rnd 1: with **2.5mm** hook and **dark yellow DK** yarn, sc 6 in magic ring [6]

Rnds 2–8: sc in each st around [6]

Rnd 9: change to **lime green DK** yarn, sc in each st around [6]

Rnd 10: working in BLO, sc in each st around [6]

Rnds 11–22: sc in each st around [6]

Sl st in next st, insert chenille stem into stem, leaving 2.5cm (1in) extending. Fasten off and weave in ends. Repeat **Rnds 1–19** for the second stem and **Rnds 1–16** for the third stem. Complete **Rnds 23–25** for all three stems.

Rnd 23: join **lime green DK** yarn in a BLO from **Rnd 9**, working in BLO, 2 sc in each st around (2) [12]

Rnd 24: (sc 3, 2 sc in next st) 3 times [15]

Rnd 25: (sc 4, 2 sc in next st) 3 times [18]

Invisible fasten off, leaving a long tail. Insert the stem through the bottom of the calla lily. Using yarn needle and yarn tail, sew **Rnd 25** of stem to the calla lily (2).

LEAF (MAKE 3)

Rnd 1: with **2.5mm** hook and **lime green DK** yarn, ch 21, dc in 4th ch from hook (first 3 skipped ch sts count as dc st), dc 5, hdc 6, sc 5, 3 sc in last st, working on the other side of the foundation ch, sc 5, hdc 6, dc 5, dc + 2 hdc in last st [40]

Rnd 2: 2 sc in next st, sc 18, sc + ch 2 + sc in next st, sc 18, 2 sc in last st, sc in last st [45]

Sl st in next st, fasten off and weave in ends. Attach one leaf to the bottom of each stem (3).

Insert the calla lilies into the vase.

Leaf Chart

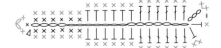

DAFFODIL BULB

Materials

- 2.5mm (C/2) crochet hook
- Paintbox Yarns Cotton DK yarn: one 50g (1¾oz) ball each of Champagne White (**cream**), Light Caramel (**tan**), Grass Green (**green**), Daffodil Yellow (**light yellow**), and Buttercup Yellow (**dark yellow**)
- Scraps of **black** and **pink** yarn
- 6mm safety eyes
- Fiberfill stuffing
- Yarn needle
- Stitch marker

Finished size

15cm (6in) tall by 6.5cm (2½in) wide

Gauge

6 sc sts and 7 rows = 2.5cm (1in)

BULB

Rnd 1: with **cream** yarn, sc 6 in magic ring [6]

Rnd 2: 2 sc in each st around [12]

Rnd 3: change to **tan** yarn, (sc 1, 2 sc in next st) 6 times [18]

Rnd 4: (sc 2, 2 sc in next st) 6 times [24]

Rnd 5: (sc 3, 2 sc in next st) 6 times [30]

Rnd 6: (sc 4, 2 sc in next st) 6 times [36]

Rnd 7: (sc 5, 2 sc in next st) 6 times [42]

Rnd 8: (sc 6, 2 sc in next st) 6 times [48]

Rnds 9–13: sc in each st around [48]

Rnd 14: (sc 3, sc2tog, sc 3) 6 times [42]

Rnd 15: (sc2tog, sc 5) 6 times [36]

Rnd 16: (sc 2, sc2tog, sc 2) 6 times [30]

Place 6mm safety eyes between **Rnds 10 and 11**, with 5 sts in between. Begin to stuff with fiberfill.

Rnd 17: (sc2tog, sc 3) 6 times [24]

Rnd 18: sc in each st around [24]

Rnd 19: (sc 1, sc2tog, sc 1) 6 times [18]

Rnd 20: sc in each st around [18]

Rnd 21: (sc2tog, sc 1) 6 times [12]

Rnd 22: change to **green** yarn, working in BLO, sc in each st around [12]

Rnd 23: working in BLO, (sc2tog, sc 2) 3 times [9]

Rnds 24–25: sc in each st around [9]

Rnd 26: (sc2tog, sc 1) 3 times [6]

Rnds 27–30: sc in each st around [6]

Finish stuffing. Fasten off, leaving a long tail. With a yarn needle, weave tail through FLO to close opening. Weave in ends. Stitch on mouth and cheeks using **black** and **pink** yarn (see Making Up: Stitching Facial Details).

Rnd 31: join **green** yarn in any front loop from **Rnd 23**, (ch 8, sl st in 2nd ch from hook, sc 1, hdc 5, sl st in next 2 sts from **Rnd 23**, ch 10, sl st in 2nd ch from hook, sc 1, hdc 7, sl st in next st from **Rnd 23**) 3 times [6 leaves]

Fasten off and weave in ends.

Rnd 32: join **tan** yarn in any front loop from **Rnd 22**, (sc 3, 2 sc in next st) 3 times [15]

Rnd 33: sc in each st around [15]

Fasten off and weave in ends. Tie short lengths of **cream** yarn to **Rnds 1 and 2**. Cut them all the same length and unravel yarn to make it fuzzy.

DAFFODIL

Rnd 1: with **dark yellow** yarn, sc 6 in magic ring [6]

Rnd 2: working in FLO, 2 sc in each st around [12]

Rnd 3: (sc 3, 2 sc in next st) 3 times [15]

Rnd 4: (sc 4, 2 sc in next st) 3 times [18]

Fasten off and weave in ends.

Rnd 5: join **light yellow** yarn in any back loop from **Rnd 2**, (ch 7, sc in 2nd ch from hook, sc 5, sc in next st from **Rnd 2**) 6 times [42]

Rnd 6: (dc 4, hdc 1, sc 1, sl st 1, sc 1, hdc 1, dc 4, sl st 1) 6 times [6 petals]

Fasten off and weave in ends.
Attach daffodil to top of bulb.

HONEY BEE

Materials

- 2.5mm (C/2) crochet hook
- Paintbox Yarns Cotton DK yarn: one 50g (1¾oz) ball each of Pure Black (**black**), Daffodil Yellow (**yellow**), and Paper White (**white**)
- 5mm safety eyes
- Fiberfill stuffing
- Yarn needle
- Stitch marker

Finished size

5cm (2in) tall by 5cm (2in) wide

Gauge

6 sc sts and 7 rows = 2.5cm (1in)

ANTENNA (MAKE 2)

Rnd 1: with **black** yarn, ch 6, working in back bump loops, sc in 2nd ch from hook, sl st in next 4 ch sts [5]

Fasten off and do not weave in ends.

BODY

Rnd 1: with **yellow** yarn, sc 5 in magic ring [5]

Rnd 2: 2 sc in each st around [10]

Rnd 3: (sc 1, 2 sc in next st) 5 times [15]

Rnd 4: (sc 2, 2 sc in next st) 5 times [20]

Rnd 5: sc in each st around [20]

Rnd 6: change to **black** yarn, sc in each st around [20]

Rnd 7: change to **yellow** yarn, sc in each st around [20]

Rnd 8: sc in each st around [20]

Rnd 9: change to **black** yarn, sc in each st around [20]

Rnd 10: change to **yellow** yarn, sc in each st around [20]

Place 5mm safety eyes between **Rnds 3 and 4**, with 5 sts in between. Attach antennae between **Rnds 5 and 6**, with 2 sts in between. Begin to stuff with fiberfill.

Rnd 11: (sc2tog, sc 2) 5 times [15]

Rnd 12: (sc2tog, sc 1) 5 times [10]

Rnd 13: sc in each st around [10]

Rnd 14: (sc2tog) 5 times [5]

Finish stuffing. Fasten off, leaving a long yarn tail. With a yarn needle, weave the tail through FLO to close the opening. Weave in all ends.

WING (MAKE 2)

Rnd 1: with **white** yarn, sc 5 in magic ring [5]

Rnd 2: 2 sc in each st around [10]

Rnd 3: (sc 1, 2 sc in next st) repeat 5 times [15]

Sl st in next st. Invisible fasten off (see Finishing: Invisible Fasten Off) and weave in ends. Attach the wings to the top of the honey bee.

SUNFLOWER

Materials

- 3.5mm (E/4) crochet hook
- Paintbox Yarns Cotton Aran yarn: one 50g (1¾oz) ball each of Buttercup Yellow (**dark yellow**), Champagne White (**cream**), Soft Fudge (**brown**), and Grass Green (**green**)
- Scrap of **black** yarn
- 6mm safety eyes
- Fiberfill stuffing
- 16-gauge floral wire
- Yarn needle
- Stitch marker

Finished size

19cm (7½in) tall by 12.5cm (5in) wide

Gauge

5 sc sts and 6 rows = 2.5cm (1in)

POT

Rnd 1: with **dark yellow** yarn, sc 6 in magic ring [6]

Rnd 2: 2 sc in each st around [12]

Rnd 3: (sc 1, 2 sc in next st) 6 times [18]

Rnd 4: (sc 2, 2 sc in next st) 6 times [24]

Rnd 5: (sc 3, 2 sc in next st) 6 times [30]

Rnd 6: (sc 4, 2 sc in next st) 6 times [36]

Rnd 7: (sc 5, 2 sc in next st) 6 times [42]

Rnd 8: working in BLO, sc in each st around [42]

Rnds 9–13: sc in each st around [42]

Rnd 14: (sc 6, 2 sc in next st) 6 times [48]

Rnd 15: sc in each st around [48]

Rnd 16: change to **cream** yarn, sc in each st around [48]

Rnd 17: sc in each st around [48]

Begin to stuff with fiberfill. Do not finish off and cut yarn. Make the dirt before moving on to **Rnd 18.**

Rnd 18: place the dirt in the pot and line up the stitches from **Rnd 17** of the pot and **Rnd 8** of the dirt. With the yarn used to make the pot, sc in each st around, working in both loops of both pieces to join them together (see Making Up: Crocheting Two Pieces Together) [48]

Rnd 19: ch 1, sc in each st around, join with sl st in first st [48]

Rnd 20: sl st in each st around [48]

Invisible fasten off (see Finishing: Invisible Fasten Off) and weave in ends. Begin shaping by inserting needle from center bottom to center top, then take needle back down from center top to slightly off center bottom and back up to center top. Pull to create an indentation in the bottom of the pot. Fasten off and weave in ends.

DIRT

Rnd 1: with **brown** yarn, sc 6 in magic ring [6]

Rnd 2: 2 sc in each st around [12]

Rnd 3: (sc 1, 2 sc in next st) 6 times [18]

Rnd 4: (sc 2, 2 sc in next st) 6 times [24]

Rnd 5: (sc 3, 2 sc in next st) 6 times [30]

Rnd 6: (sc 4, 2 sc in next st) 6 times [36]

Rnd 7: (sc 5, 2 sc in next st) 6 times [42]

Rnd 8: (sc 6, 2 sc in next st) 6 times [48]

Invisible fasten off and weave in ends.

CENTER AND STEM

Rnd 1: with **brown** yarn, sc 6 in magic ring [6]

Rnd 2: 2 sc in each st around [12]

Rnd 3: (sc 1, 2 sc in next st) 6 times [18]

Rnd 4: (sc 2, 2 sc in next st) 6 times [24]

Rnd 5: (sc 3, 2 sc in next st) 6 times [30]

Rnd 6: sc in each st around [30]

Rnd 7: working in BLO, sc in each st around [30]

Rnd 8: change to **green** yarn, working in BLO, sc in each st around [30]

Insert 6mm safety eyes between **Rnds 2 and 3**, with 6 sts in between. Add stitches for the mouth, using **black** yarn (see Making Up: Stitching Facial Details). Begin stuffing with fiberfill.

Rnd 9: (sc2tog, sc 3) 6 times [24]

Rnd 10: (sc2tog, sc 2) 6 times [18]

Rnd 11: (sc2tog, sc 1) 6 times [12]

Rnd 12: sc in each st around [12]

Rnd 13: (sc2tog, sc 2) 3 times [9]

Rnds 14–15: sc in each st around [9]

Rnd 16: (sc2tog, sc 1) 3 times [6]

Rnds 17–27: sc in each st around [6]

Fasten off, leaving a long yarn tail. Stuff stem with fiberfill and insert floral wire into stem, leaving 4cm (1½in) extending past the stem. Insert the stem into the center of the dirt. With a yarn needle and yarn tail, sew **Rnd 27** of the stem to the dirt.

PETAL (MAKE 20)

Rnd 1: with **dark yellow** yarn, sc 5 in magic ring [5]

Rnd 2: sc in each st around [5]

Rnd 3: 2 sc in each st around [10]

Rnds 4–7: sc in each st around [10]

Rnd 8: (sc2tog) repeat 5 times [5]

Fasten off, leaving a long yarn tail. With yarn needle and yarn tail, sew **Rnd 8** of the petal together, then sew ten of the petals to the front loops from **Rnd 8** of the sunflower. Sew the remaining ten petals to the front loops from **Rnd 7** of the sunflower. Bend the stem so that the weight of the petals does not tip the pot over.

PETAL LEAF (MAKE 2)

Rnd 1: with **green** yarn, ch 10, sl st in 2nd ch from hook, sc 1, hdc 1, dc 4, hdc 1, sc 3 in last ch, working on the other side of the foundation ch, hdc 1, dc 4, hdc 1, sc 1, sl st 1, sl st in beginning skipped ch st [20]

Invisible fasten off and weave in ends. Attach to the dirt on either side of the stem.

Leaf Chart

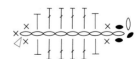

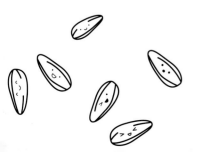

GREEN

A complex chemical called chlorophyll gives plants their green color. Many shades of green have been named after plants or are related to plants, such as moss, forest, lime, sage, and mint.

BARREL CACTUS

Materials

- 3.5mm (E/4) crochet hook
- Paintbox Yarns Cotton Aran yarn: one 50g (1¾oz) ball each of Racing Green (**dark green**), Champagne White (**cream**), Soft Fudge (**brown**), Grass Green (**green**) and Bubblegum Pink (**pink**)
- Scrap of **black** yarn
- 8mm safety eyes
- Fiberfill stuffing
- Yarn needle
- Stitch marker

Finished size

16.5cm (6½in) tall by 9cm (3½in) wide

Gauge

5 sc sts and 6 rows = 2.5cm (1in)

POT

Rnd 1: with **dark green** yarn, sc 6 in magic ring [6]

Rnd 2: 2 sc in each st around [12]

Rnd 3: (sc 1, 2 sc in next st) 6 times [18]

Rnd 4: (sc 2, 2 sc in next st) 6 times [24]

Rnd 5: (sc 3, 2 sc in next st) 6 times [30]

Rnd 6: (sc 4, 2 sc in next st) 6 times [36]

Rnd 7: (sc 5, 2 sc in next st) 6 times [42]

Rnd 8: working in BLO, sc in each st around [42]

Rnds 9–13: sc in each st around [42]

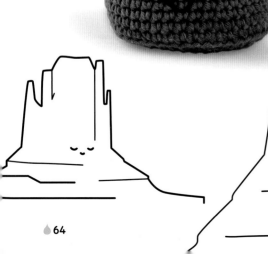

Rnd 14: (sc 6, 2 sc in next st) 6 times [48]

Rnd 15: sc in each st around [48]

Rnd 16: change to **cream** yarn, sc in each st around [48]

Rnd 17: sc in each st around [48]

Place 8mm safety eyes between **Rnds 13 and 14**, with 5 sts in between. Begin to stuff with fiberfill. Do not finish off and cut yarn. Make the dirt before moving on to **Rnd 18**.

Rnd 18: place the dirt in the pot and line up the stitches from **Rnd 17** of the pot and **Rnd 8** of the dirt. With the yarn used to make the pot, sc in each st around, working in both loops of both pieces to join them together (see Making Up: Crocheting Two Pieces Together) [48]

Rnd 19: ch 1, sc in each st around, join with sl st in first st [48]

Rnd 20: sl st in each st around [48]

Invisible fasten off (see Finishing: Invisible Fasten Off) and weave in ends. Add stitches for the mouth and cheeks using **black** and **pink** yarn (see Making Up: Stitching Facial Details). Begin shaping by inserting needle from center bottom to center top, then take needle back down from center top to slightly off center bottom and back up to center top. Pull to create an indentation in the bottom of the pot. Fasten off and weave in ends.

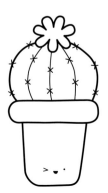

DIRT

Rnd 1: with **brown** yarn, sc 6 in magic ring [6]

Rnd 2: 2 sc in each st around [12]

Rnd 3: (sc 1, 2 sc in next st) 6 times [18]

Rnd 4: (sc 2, 2 sc in next st) 6 times [24]

Rnd 5: (sc 3, 2 sc in next st) 6 times [30]

Rnd 6: (sc 4, 2 sc in next st) 6 times [36]

Rnd 7: (sc 5, 2 sc in next st) 6 times [42]

Rnd 8: (sc 6, 2 sc in next st) 6 times [48]

Invisible fasten off and weave in ends.

CACTUS

Row 1: with **green** yarn, ch 18, sc in 2nd ch from hook, sc 16, turn [17]

Row 2: working in BLO, ch 1, sc in each st across, turn [17]

Rows 3–27: repeat **Row 2**

Row 28: roll the crochet fabric into a cylinder and line up the stitches from **Row 1 and Row 27** of the cactus. Sl st in each st across, working in both loops of both pieces to join them together (see Making Up: Crocheting Two Pieces Together) [17]

Fasten off, leaving a long yarn tail. With a yarn needle, weave in and out of the side loops of one of the ends of the cylinder and pull yarn to cinch it closed. Stuff the cactus with fiberfill stuffing. Weave in and out of the side loops of the open end and close it up.

Sew the cactus to the the dirt. Using **cream** yarn, add prickles by pulling and knotting small pieces of yarn through the FLO from **Rows 1–27**.

FLOWER (MAKE 3)

Rnd 1: with **pink** yarn, sc 5 in magic ring [5]

Rnd 2: (sl st + ch 2 + dc 1 + ch 2 + sl st) 5 times [5 petals]

Fasten off and weave in ends. Attach the flowers to the top of the cactus.

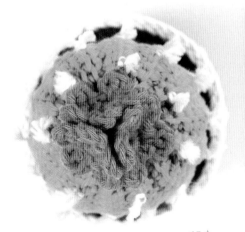

CLOVER

Materials

- 3.5mm (E/4) and 2.5mm (C/2) crochet hooks
- Paintbox Yarns Cotton Aran yarn: one 50g (1¾oz) ball each of Vanilla Cream (**cream)** and Soft Fudge (**brown)**
- Paintbox Yarns Cotton DK yarn: one 50g (1¾oz) ball of Grass Green (**green)**
- Scraps of **black** and **pink** yarn
- 7mm safety eyes
- Fiberfill stuffing
- 26-gauge floral wire
- Yarn needle
- Stitch marker

Finished size

9cm (3½in) tall by 9cm (3½in) wide

Gauge

5 sc sts and 6 rows = 2.5cm (1in) using Aran yarn

6 sc sts and 7 rows = 2.5cm (1in) using DK yarn

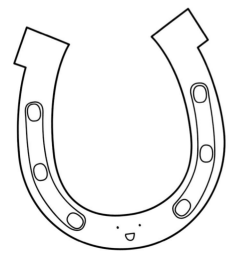

POT

Rnd 1: with **3.5mm** hook and **cream Aran** yarn, sc 6 in magic ring [6]

Rnd 2: 2 sc in each st around [12]

Rnd 3: (sc 1, 2 sc in next st) 6 times [18]

Rnd 4: (sc 2, 2 sc in next st) 6 times [24]

Rnd 5: (sc 3, 2 sc in next st) 6 times [30]

Rnd 6: (sc 4, 2 sc in next st) 6 times [36]

Rnd 7: working in BLO, sc in each st around [36]

Rnds 8–11: sc in each st around [36]

Rnd 12: (sc 5, 2 sc in next st) 6 times [42]

Rnds 13–15: sc in each st around [42]

Place 7mm safety eyes between **Rnds 11 and 12**, with 4 sts in between. Begin to stuff with fiberfill. Do not finish off and cut yarn. Make the dirt before moving on to **Rnd 16**.

Rnd 16: place the dirt in the pot and line up the stitches from **Rnd 15** of the pot and **Rnd 7** of the dirt. With the yarn used to make the pot, sc in each st around, working in both loops of both pieces to join them together (see Making Up: Crocheting Two Pieces Together) [42]

Rnd 17: ch 1, sc in each st around, join with sl st in first st [42]

Rnd 18: sl st in each st around [42]

Invisible fasten off (see Finishing: Invisible Fasten Off) and weave in ends. Add stitches for the mouth and cheeks using **black** and **pink** yarn (see Making Up: Stitching Facial Details). Begin shaping by inserting needle from center bottom to center top, then take needle back down from center top to slightly off center bottom and back up to center top. Pull to create an indentation in the bottom of the pot. Fasten off and weave in ends.

DIRT

Rnd 1: with **3.5mm** hook and **brown Aran** yarn, sc 6 in magic ring [6]

Rnd 2: 2 sc in each st around [12]

Rnd 3: (sc 1, 2 sc in next st) 6 times [18]

Rnd 4: (sc 2, 2 sc in next st) 6 times [24]

Rnd 5: (sc 3, 2 sc in next st) 6 times [30]

Rnd 6: (sc 4, 2 sc in next st) 6 times [36]

Rnd 7: (sc 5, 2 sc in next st) 6 times [42]

Invisible fasten off and weave in ends.

CLOVER LEAF (MAKE 12)

Rnd 1: cut a 7.5-cm (3-in) piece of floral wire. With **2.5mm** hook and **green DK** yarn, (ch 4 + 2 tr + hdc + 2 tr + ch 4) 3 times in magic ring, ch 5, hold wire behind the foundation ch and crochet the following sts around the wire (see Making Up: Crocheting with Floral Wire): sc in 2nd ch from hook, sc in next 3 ch sts, sl st in magic ring [43]

Fasten off and weave in ends (1).

Insert the clover into the dirt.

YOU'RE MY LUCKY CHARM...

Make a 4-leaf clover instead of just a 3-leaf by repeating the beginning Clover Leaf instructions four times instead of just three.

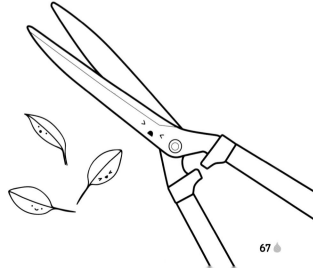

FERN

Materials

- 3.5mm (E/4) and 2.5mm (C/2) crochet hooks
- Paintbox Yarns Cotton Aran yarn: one 50g (1¾oz) ball each of Lime Green (**lime green**) and Soft Fudge (**brown**)
- Paintbox Yarns Cotton DK yarn: one 50g (1¾oz) ball of Grass Green (**green**)
- Scraps of **black** and **pink** yarn
- 7mm safety eyes
- Fiberfill stuffing
- Yarn needle
- Stitch marker

Finished size

9cm (3½in) tall by 9cm (3½in) wide

Gauge

5 sc sts and 6 rows = 2.5cm (1in) using Aran yarn

6 sc sts and 7 rows = 2.5cm (1in) using DK yarn

POT

Rnd 1: with **3.5mm** hook and **lime green Aran** yarn, sc 6 in magic ring [6]

Rnd 2: 2 sc in each st around [12]

Rnd 3: (sc 1, 2 sc in next st) 6 times [18]

Rnd 4: (sc 2, 2 sc in next st) 6 times [24]

Rnd 5: (sc 3, 2 sc in next st) 6 times [30]

Rnd 6: (sc 4, 2 sc in next st) 6 times [36]

Rnd 7: working in BLO, sc in each st around [36]

Rnds 8–11: sc in each st around [36]

Rnd 12: (sc 5, 2 sc in next st) 6 times [42]

Rnds 13–15: sc in each st around [42]

Place 7mm safety eyes between **Rnds 11 and 12**, with 4 sts in between. Begin to stuff with fiberfill. Do not finish off and cut yarn. Make the dirt before moving on to **Rnd 16**.

Rnd 16: place the dirt in the pot and line up the stitches from **Rnd 15** of the pot and **Rnd 7** of the dirt. With the yarn used to make the pot, sc in each st around, working in both loops of both pieces to join them together (see Making Up: Crocheting Two Pieces Together) [42]

Rnd 17: ch 1, sc in each st around, join with sl st in first st [42]

Rnd 18: sl st in each st around [42]

Invisible fasten off (see Finishing: Invisible Fasten Off) and weave in ends. Add stitches for the mouth and cheeks using **black** and **pink** yarn (see Making Up: Stitching Facial Details). Begin shaping by inserting needle from center bottom to center top, then take needle back down from center top to slightly off center bottom and back up to center top. Pull to create an indentation in the bottom of the pot. Fasten off and weave in ends.

DIRT

Rnd 1: with **3.5mm** hook and **brown Aran** yarn, sc 6 in magic ring [6]

Rnd 2: 2 sc in each st around [12]

Rnd 3: (sc 1, 2 sc in next st) 6 times [18]

Rnd 4: (sc 2, 2 sc in next st) 6 times [24]

Rnd 5: (sc 3, 2 sc in next st) 6 times [30]

Rnd 6: (sc 4, 2 sc in next st) 6 times [36]

Rnd 7: (sc 5, 2 sc in next st) 6 times [42]

Invisible fasten off and weave in ends.

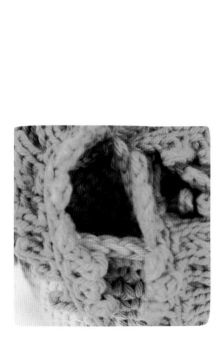

SO FERNY...

How do plants contact each other? They use the te-leaf-one! How do plants make themselves heard? With amp-leaf-ication!

FERN (MAKE 7)

Start with a 15cm (6in) yarn tail when making the slip knot.

Rnd 1: with **2.5mm hook** and **green DK** yarn, ch 24, sl st in 2nd ch from hook, sl st 2, (ch 3, sl st in 2nd ch from hook, sl st 1, sl st 2 in foundation ch) 2 times, (ch 4, sl st in 2nd ch from hook, sl st 2, sl st 2 in foundation ch) 2 times, (ch 5, sl st in 2nd ch from hook, sl st 3, sl st 2 in foundation ch) 2 times, (ch 6, sl st in 2nd ch from hook, sl st 4, sl st 2 in foundation ch) 3 times, sl st 2, ch 2, working on the other side of the foundation ch, sl st 4, (ch 6, sl st in 2nd ch from hook, sl st 4, sl st 2 in foundation ch) 3 times, (ch 5, sl st in 2nd ch from hook, sl st 3, sl st 2 in foundation ch) 2 times, (ch 4, sl st in 2nd ch from hook, sl st 2, sl st 2 in foundation ch) 2 times, (ch 3, sl st in 2nd ch from hook, sl st 1, sl st 2 in foundation ch) 2 times [113]

Fasten off and weave in end, leaving beginning yarn tail (1). With a yarn needle and beginning yarn tail, sew fern leaves to dirt (2).

LET LOVE GROW...

When your fern is complete add a tag that says, "Be-leaf in yourself because you are so fern-tastic!"

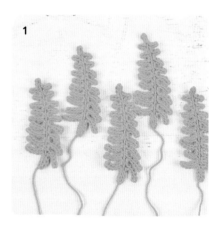

CaTeRPiLLAR

Materials

- 2.5mm (C/2) crochet hook
- Paintbox Yarns Cotton DK yarn: one 50g (1¾oz) ball each of Spearmint Green (**green**) and Lime (**lime green**)
- Scrap of **black** yarn
- 6mm safety eyes
- Fiberfill stuffing
- Yarn needle
- Stitch marker

Finished size

2.5cm (1in) tall by 9cm (3½in) wide

Gauge

6 sc sts and 7 rows = 2.5cm (1in)

ANTENNA (MAKE 2)

Rnd 1: with **black** yarn, ch 6, working in back bump loops, sc in 2nd ch from hook, sl st in next 4 ch sts [5]

Fasten off and do not weave in ends.

BODY

Rnd 1: with **green** yarn, sc 5 in magic ring [5]

Rnd 2: 2 sc in each st around [10]

Rnd 3: (sc 1, 2 sc in next st) 5 times [15]

Rnds 4–5: sc in each st around [15]

Rnd 6: change to **lime green** yarn, (sc 2, 2 sc in next st) 5 times [20]

Rnd 7: working in BLO, sc 2, 3-dc-bl, sc 15, 3-dc-bl, sc 1 [20]

Place 6mm safety eyes between **Rnds 3 and 4** on the top half of the body, with 5 sts in between. Attach antennae between **Rnds 5 and 6**, with 1 st in between. Begin to stuff with fiberfill.

Rnd 8: change to **green** yarn, working in BLO, sc in each st around [20]

Rnds 9–10: working in BLO, sc in each st around [20]

Rnd 11: change to **lime green** yarn, working in BLO, sc in each st around [20]

Rnd 12: working in BLO, sc 2, 3-dc-bl, sc 15, 3-dc-bl, sc 1 [20]

Rnds 13–22: repeat **Rnds 8–12** twice

Rnd 23: join **green** yarn, working in BLO, sc in each st around [20]

Rnd 24: working in BLO, (sc2tog, sc 2) 5 times [15]

Rnd 25: working in BLO, (sc2tog, sc 1) 5 times [10]

Rnd 26: working in BLO, (sc2tog) 5 times [5]

Finish stuffing. Fasten off, leaving a long yarn tail. With a yarn needle, weave the tail through FLO to close the opening. Weave in all ends.

WATERING CAN

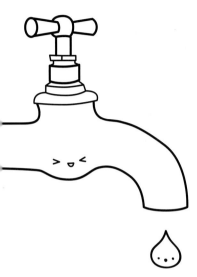

Materials

- 3.5mm (E/4) crochet hook
- Paintbox Yarns Cotton Aran yarn: one 50g (1¾oz) ball each of Grass Green (**green**) and Kingfisher Blue (**blue**)
- Scraps of **black** and **pink** yarn
- 8mm safety eyes
- Fiberfill stuffing
- Chenille stem (pipe cleaner)
- Yarn needle
- Stitch marker

Finished size

10cm (4in) tall by 18cm (7in) wide

Gauge

5 sc sts and 6 rows = 2.5cm (1in)

CAN

Rnd 1: with **green** yarn, sc 7 in magic ring [7]

Rnd 2: 2 sc in each st around [14]

Rnd 3: (sc 1, 2 sc in next st) 7 times [21]

Rnd 4: (sc 2, 2 sc in next st) 7 times [28]

Rnd 5: (sc 3, 2 sc in next st) 7 times [35]

Rnd 6: (sc 4, 2 sc in next st) 7 times [42]

Rnd 7: (sc 5, 2 sc in next st) times [49]

Rnd 8: working in BLO, sc in each st around [49]

Rnds 9–12: sc in each st around [49]

Rnd 13: (sc2tog, sc 5) 7 times [42]

Rnds 14–16: sc in each st around [42]

Rnd 17: (sc2tog, sc 5) 6 times [36]

Rnds 18–20: sc in each st around [36]

Place 8mm safety eyes between **Rnds 14 and 15**, with 5 sts in between. Begin to stuff with fiberfill. Do not finish off and cut yarn. Make the water before moving on to **Rnd 21**.

Rnd 21: place the water in the can and line up the stitches from **Rnd 20** of the can and **Rnd 6** of the water. With the yarn used to make the can, sc in each st around, working in both loops of both pieces to join them together (see Making Up: Crocheting Two Pieces Together) [36]

Rnd 22: ch 1, sc in each st around, join with sl st in first st [36]

Rnd 23: sl st in each st around [36]

Invisible fasten off (see Finishing: Invisible Fasten Off) and weave in ends. Add stitches for the mouth and cheeks using **black** and **pink** yarn (see Making Up: Stitching Facial Details). Begin shaping by inserting needle from center bottom to center top, then take needle back down from center top to slightly off center bottom and back up to center top. Pull to create an indentation in the bottom of the can. Fasten off and weave in ends.

WATER

Rnd 1: with **blue** yarn, sc 6 in magic ring [6]

Rnd 2: 2 sc in each st around [12]

Rnd 3: (sc 1, 2 sc in next st) 6 times [18]

Rnd 4: (sc 2, 2 sc in next st) 6 times [24]

Rnd 5: (sc 3, 2 sc in next st) 6 times [30]

Rnd 6: (sc 4, 2 sc in next st) 6 times [36]

Invisible fasten off and weave in ends.

UPPER PART

Rnd 1: with **green** yarn, sc 6 in magic ring [6]

Rnd 2: 2 sc in each st around [12]

Rnd 3: (sc 1, 2 sc in next st) 6 times [18]

Rnd 4: (sc 2, 2 sc in next st) 6 times [24]

Rnd 5: (sc 3, 2 sc in next st) 6 times [30]

Rnd 6: (sc 4, 2 sc in next st) 6 times [36]

Fasten off, leaving a long yarn tail. Fold the upper part in half and sew the two sides together with a yarn needle and yarn tail.

SPOUT

Rnd 1: with **green** yarn, sc 7 in magic ring [7]

Rnd 2: 2 sc in each st around [14]

Rnd 3: (sc 1, 2 sc in next st) 7 times [21]

Rnd 4: working in BLO, sc in each st around [21]

Rnd 5: (sc2tog, sc 1) 7 times [14]

Rnd 6: (sc2tog) 7 times [7]

Rnd 7: sc in each st around [7]

Rnd 8: sc 6, 2 sc in next st [8]

Rnd 9: (sc 3, 2 sc in next st) 2 times [10]

Rnd 10: sc in each st around [10]

Rnd 11: (sc 4, 2 sc in next st) 2 times [12]

Rnd 12: sc in each st around, turn [12]

Rnd 13: ch 1, sc 6, leave remaining sts unworked [6]

Fasten off, leaving a long yarn tail.

HANDLE

Rnd 1: with **green** yarn, sc 6 in magic ring [6]

Rnds 2–14: sc in each st around [6]

Fasten off, leaving a long yarn tail. Insert a chenille stem into the handle and bend it into the shape of a "U". With a yarn needle and yarn tail, sew the upper part to the top half of the watering can, the handle to **Rnds 12 and 22** of the side of the watering can, and the spout to **Rnds 10–15** of the side of the watering can. Weave in ends.

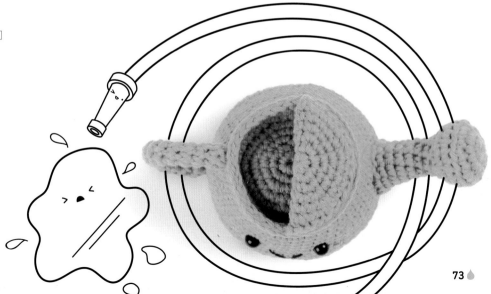

Blue is one of the rarest of colors in nature. Even the few plants that appear blue do not actually contain the color— they have simply developed some unique features that use the physics of light.

CROCUS BULB

Materials

- 2.5mm (C/2) crochet hook
- Paintbox Yarns Cotton DK yarn: one 50g (1¾oz) ball each of Champagne White (**cream**), Light Caramel (**tan**), Grass Green (**green**), Daffodil Yellow (**yellow**), Duck Egg Blue (**light blue**), and Dolphin Blue (**dark blue**)
- Scraps of **black** and **pink** yarn
- 6mm safety eyes
- Fiberfill stuffing
- Yarn needle
- Stitch marker

Finished size

15cm (6in) tall by 6.5cm (2½in) wide

Gauge

6 sc sts and 7 rows = 2.5cm (1in)

BULB

Rnd 1: with **cream** yarn, sc 6 in magic ring [6]

Rnd 2: 2 sc in each st around [12]

Rnd 3: change to **tan** yarn, (sc 1, 2 sc in next st) 6 times [18]

Rnd 4: (sc 2, 2 sc in next st) 6 times [24]

Rnd 5: (sc 3, 2 sc in next st) 6 times [30]

Rnd 6: (sc 4, 2 sc in next st) 6 times [36]

Rnd 7: (sc 5, 2 sc in next st) 6 times [42]

Rnd 8: (sc 6, 2 sc in next st) 6 times [48]

Rnds 9–13: sc in each st around [48]

Rnd 14: (sc 3, sc2tog, sc 3) 6 times [42]

Rnd 15: (sc2tog, sc 5) repeat 6 times [36]

Rnd 16: (sc 2, sc2tog, sc 2) repeat 6 times [30]

Place 6mm safety eyes between **Rnds 10 and 11**, with 5 sts in between. Begin to stuff with fiberfill.

Rnd 17: (sc2tog, sc 3) 6 times [24]

Rnd 18: sc in each st around [24]

Rnd 19: (sc 1, sc2tog, sc 1) 6 times [18]

Rnd 20: sc in each st around [18]

Rnd 21: (sc2tog, sc 1) 6 times [12]

Rnd 22: change to **green** yarn, working in BLO, sc in each st around [12]

Rnd 23: working in BLO, (sc2tog, sc 2) 3 times [9]

Rnds 24–27: sc in each st around [9]

Rnd 28: working in BLO, sc in each st around [9]

Rnd 29: working in BLO, (sc2tog, sc 1) 3 times [6]

Finish stuffing. Fasten off, leaving a long yarn tail. With a yarn needle, weave the tail through FLO to close the opening. Weave in all ends. Add stitches for the mouth and cheeks using **black** and **pink** yarn (see Making Up: Stitching Facial Details).

Rnd 30: join **yellow** yarn in any front loop from **Rnd 29**, (sl st, ch 8, sl st in 2nd ch from hook, sl st in next 6 ch sts, sl st in next st from **Rnd 29**) 3 times [27]

Fasten off and weave in ends. Tie short lengths of **cream** yarn to **Rnds 1 and 2**. Cut them all the same length and unravel yarn to make it fuzzy (1).

Make and sew on the petals before moving on to **Rnd 31**.

Rnd 31: join **green** yarn in any front loop from **Rnd 23**, (sl st, ch 8, sl st in 2nd ch from hook, sc 1, hdc 5, sl st in next 2 sts from **Rnd 23**, ch 10, sl st in 2nd ch from hook, sc 1, hdc 7, sl st in next st from **Rnd 23**) 3 times [60]

Fasten off and weave in ends.

Rnd 32: join **tan** yarn in any front loop from **Rnd 22**, (sc 3, 2 sc in next st) 3 times [15]

Rnd 33: sc in each st around [15]

Fasten off and weave in ends.

PETAL (MAKE 6—3 LIGHT BLUE AND 3 DARK BLUE)

Rnd 1: with **light** or **dark blue** yarn as required, ch 10, sc in 2nd ch from hook, sc 2, hdc 3, dc 2, 5 dc in last st, working on the other side of the foundation ch, dc 2, hdc 3, sc 3 [21]

Fasten off, leaving a long yarn tail. Make three petals in **light blue** yarn and three petals in **dark blue** yarn (2).

Sew the light blue petals to the front loops from **Rnd 29** of the bulb and the dark blue petals to the front loops from **Rnd 28**.

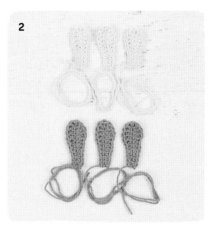

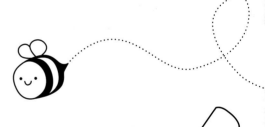

HOCUS CROCUS...

The surest sign that spring is nigh is the sudden appearance of crocus blooms; so, the cheer-up power of this crochet version is sure to be magical!

DELPHINIUM

Materials

- 3.5mm (E/4) and 2.5mm (C/2) crochet hooks
- Paintbox Yarns Cotton Aran yarn: one 50g (1¾oz) ball each of Duck Egg Blue (**light blue**) and Soft Fudge (**brown**)
- Paintbox Yarns Cotton DK yarn: one 50g (1¾oz) ball each of Grass Green (**green**), Duck Egg Blue (**light blue**), and Dolphin Blue (**dark blue**)
- Scraps of **black** and **pink** yarn
- 7mm safety eyes
- Fiberfill stuffing
- Yarn needle
- Stitch marker

Finished size

16.5cm (6½in) tall by 7.5cm (3in) wide

Gauge

5 sc sts and 6 rows = 2.5cm (1in) using Aran yarn

6 sc sts and 7 rows = 2.5cm (1in) using DK yarn

POT

Rnd 1: with **3.5mm** hook and **light blue Aran** yarn, sc 6 in magic ring [6]

Rnd 2: 2 sc in each st around [12]

Rnd 3: (sc 1, 2 sc in next st) 6 times [18]

Rnd 4: (sc 2, 2 sc in next st) 6 times [24]

Rnd 5: (sc 3, 2 sc in next st) 6 times [30]

Rnd 6: (sc 4, 2 sc in next st) 6 times [36]

Rnd 7: working in BLO, sc in each st around [36]

Rnds 8–11: sc in each st around [36]

Rnd 12: (sc 5, 2 sc in next st) 6 times [42]

Rnds 13–15: sc in each st around [42]

Place 7mm safety eyes between **Rnds 11 and 12**, with 4 sts in between. Begin to stuff with fiberfill. Do not finish off and cut yarn. Make the dirt before moving on to **Rnd 16**.

Rnd 16: place the dirt in the pot and line up the stitches from **Rnd 15** of the pot and **Rnd 7** of the dirt. With the yarn used to make the pot, sc in each st around, working in both loops of both pieces to join them together (see Making Up: Crocheting Two Pieces Together) [42]

Rnd 17: ch 1, sc in each st around, join with sl st in first st [42]

Rnd 18: sl st in each st around [42]

Invisible fasten off (see Finishing: Invisible Fasten Off) and weave in ends. Add stitches for the mouth and cheeks using **black** and **pink** yarn (see Making Up: Stitching Facial Details). Begin shaping by inserting needle from center bottom to center top, then take needle back down from center top to slightly off center bottom and back up to center top. Pull to create an indentation in the bottom of the pot. Fasten off and weave in ends.

DIRT

Rnd 1: with **3.5mm** hook and **brown Aran** yarn, sc 6 in magic ring [6]

Rnd 2: 2 sc in each st around [12]

Rnd 3: (sc 1, 2 sc in next st) 6 times [18]

Rnd 4: (sc 2, 2 sc in next st) 6 times [24]

Rnd 5: (sc 3, 2 sc in next st) 6 times [30]

Rnd 6: (sc 4, 2 sc in next st) 6 times [36]

Rnd 7: (sc 5, 2 sc in next st) 6 times [42]

Invisible fasten off and weave in ends.

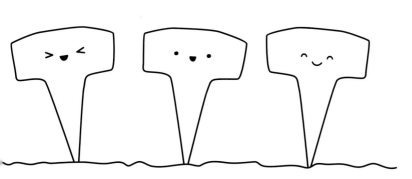

STEM

Rnd 1: with **2.5mm** hook and **green DK** yarn, sc 6 in magic ring [6]

Rnds 2–3: sc in each st around [6]

Rnd 4: (sc 2, 2 sc in next st) 2 times [8]

Rnds 5–6: sc in each st around [8]

Rnd 7: (sc 3, 2 sc in next st) 2 times [10]

Rnds 8–9: sc in each st around [10]

Rnd 10: (sc 4, 2 sc in next st) 2 times [12]

Rnds 11–13: sc in each st around [12]

Rnd 14: (sc 5, 2 sc in next st) 2 times [14]

Rnds 15–17: sc in each st around [14]

Fasten off, leaving a long yarn tail. Stuff with fiberfill. With a yarn needle and yarn tail, sew **Rnd 17** of the stem between **Rnds 2 and 3** of the dirt (1).

FLOWER (MAKE 11)

Rnd 1: with **2.5mm** hook and **light blue DK** yarn, sc 5 in magic ring [5]

Rnd 2: change to **dark blue** yarn, (sl st + ch 3 + 2 tr + ch 3 + sl st in next st) 5 times [5 petals]

Fasten off and weave in ends. Attach the flowers around the stem (2).

BUD (MAKE 5)

Rnd 1: with **2.5mm** hook and **light blue DK** yarn, sc 5 in magic ring [5]

Rnd 2: 2 sc in each st around [10]

Rnds 3–4: sc in each st around [10]

Rnd 5: (sc2tog) 5 times [5]

Fasten off and weave in ends. Attach the buds around the top of the stem.

LEAF (MAKE 2)

Rnd 1: with **2.5mm** hook and **green DK** yarn, sc 6 in magic ring [6]

Rnd 2: 2 sc in each st around [12]

Rnd 3: sl st 2, ch 3, sl st in 2nd ch from hook, sc in next ch, sl st 1, ch 4, sl st in 2nd ch from hook, sc in next ch, hdc in next ch, sl st 1, ch 5, sl st in 2nd ch from hook, sc in next 2 chs, hdc in next ch, sl st 1, ch 6, sl st in 2nd ch from hook, sc in next 3 chs, hdc in next ch, sl st 1, ch 5, sl st in 2nd ch from hook, sc in next 2 chs, hdc in next ch, sl st 1, ch 4, sl st in 2nd ch from hook, sc in next ch, hdc in next ch, sl st 1, ch 3, sl st in 2nd ch from hook, sc in next ch, sl st 3, ch 5, sl st in 2nd ch from hook, sl st in next 3 chs, sl st in same st as ch 5 [39]

Fasten off and weave in ends.

Attach the leaves to the dirt.

TROWEL

Materials

- 2.5mm (C/2) crochet hook
- Paintbox Yarns Cotton DK yarn: one 50g (1¾oz) ball each of Stormy Grey (**gray**) and Washed Teal (**blue**)
- Scrap of **black** yarn
- 7mm safety eyes
- Fiberfill stuffing
- Yarn needle
- Stitch marker

Finished size

12.5cm (5in) tall
by 5cm (2in) wide

Gauge

6 sc sts and 7 rows
= 2.5cm (1in)

TROWEL

Rnd 1: with **gray** yarn, sc 9 in magic ring [9]

Rnd 2: (sc 2, 2 sc in next st) 3 times [12]

Rnd 3: (sc 3, 2 sc in next st) 3 times [15]

Rnd 4: (sc 4, 2 sc in next st) 3 times [18]

Rnd 5: (sc 5, 2 sc in next st) 3 times [21]

Rnd 6: (sc 6, 2 sc in next st) 3 times [24]

Rnd 7: (sc 7, 2 sc in next st) 3 times [27]

Rnd 8: (sc 8, 2 sc in next st) 3 times [30]

Rnds 9–17: sc in each st around [30]

Place 7mm safety eyes between **Rnds 12 and 13**, with 6 sts in between. Stuff lightly with fiberfill. Fasten off, leaving a long yarn tail. With a yarn needle and yarn tail, sew the opening closed. Add stitches for the mouth using **black** yarn (see Making Up: Stitching Facial Details).

HANDLE

Rnd 1: with **blue** yarn, sc 5 in magic ring [5]

Rnd 2: 2 sc in each st around [10]

Rnds 3–12: sc in each st around [10]

Rnd 13: change to **gray** yarn, sc in each st around [10]

Rnds 14–16: sc in each st around [10]

Stuff handle with fiberfill. Fasten off, leaving a long yarn tail. With a yarn needle and yarn tail, sew the handle to the trowel.

DAISY

Materials

- 3.5mm (E/4) crochet hook
- Paintbox Yarns Cotton Aran yarn: one 50g (1¾oz) ball each of Washed Teal (**blue**), Soft Fudge (**brown**), Daffodil Yellow (**yellow**), Grass Green (**green**), and Paper White (**white**)
- Scrap of **black** yarn
- 6mm safety eyes
- Fiberfill stuffing
- 20-gauge floral wire
- Yarn needle
- Stitch marker

Finished size

20cm (8in) tall by 11cm (4¼in) wide

Gauge

5 sc sts and 6 rows = 2.5cm (1in)

POT

Rnd 1: with **blue** yarn, sc 6 in magic ring [6]

Rnd 2: 2 sc in each st around [12]

Rnd 3: (sc 1, 2 sc in next st) 6 times [18]

Rnd 4: (sc 2, 2 sc in next st) 6 times [24]

Rnd 5: (sc 3, 2 sc in next st) 6 times [30]

Rnd 6: (sc 4, 2 sc in next st) 6 times [36]

Rnd 7: working in BLO, sc in each st around [36]

Rnds 8–11: sc in each st around [36]

Rnd 12: (sc 5, 2 sc in next st) 6 times [42]

Rnds 13–15: sc in each st around [42]

Begin to stuff with fiberfill. Do not finish off and cut yarn. Make the dirt before moving on to **Rnd 16**.

Rnd 16: place the dirt in the pot and line up the stitches from **Rnd 15** of the pot and **Rnd 7** of the dirt. With the yarn used to make the pot, sc in each st around, working in both loops of both pieces to join them together (see Making Up: Crocheting Two Pieces Together)[42]

Rnd 17: ch 1, sc in each st around, join with sl st in first st [42]

Rnd 18: sl st in each st around [42]

Invisible fasten off (see Finishing: Invisible Fasten Off) and weave in ends. Begin shaping by inserting needle from center bottom to center top, then take needle back down from center top to slightly off center bottom and back up to center top. Pull to create an indentation in the bottom of the pot. Fasten off and weave in ends.

DIRT

Rnd 1: with **brown** yarn, sc 6 in magic ring [6]

Rnd 2: 2 sc in each st around [12]

Rnd 3: (sc 1, 2 sc in next st) 6 times [18]

Rnd 4: (sc 2, 2 sc in next st) 6 times [24]

Rnd 5: (sc 3, 2 sc in next st) 6 times [30]

Rnd 6: (sc 4, 2 sc in next st) 6 times [36]

Rnd 7: (sc 5, 2 sc in next st) 6 times [42]

Invisible fasten off and weave in ends.

DAISY FLOWER CENTER AND STEM

Rnd 1: with **yellow** yarn, sc 6 in magic ring [6]

Rnd 2: 2 sc in each st around [12]

Rnd 3: (sc 1, 2 sc in next st) 6 times [18]

Rnd 4: (sc 2, 2 sc in next st) 6 times [24]

Rnd 5: sc in each st around [24]

Rnd 6: change to **green** yarn, working in BLO, sc in each st around [24]

Rnd 7: sc in each st around [24]

Place 6mm safety eyes between **Rnds 2 and 3**, with 6 sts in between. Add stitches for the mouth using **black** yarn (see Making Up: Stitching Facial Details). Begin stuffing with fiberfill.

Rnd 8: (sc2tog, sc 2) 6 times [18]

Rnd 9: (sc2tog, sc 1) 6 times [12]

Rnd 10: sc in each st around [12]

Rnd 11: (sc2tog, sc 2) 3 times [9]

Rnds 12–13: sc in each st around [9]

Rnd 14: (sc2tog, sc 1) 3 times [6]

Rnds 15–24: sc in each st around [6]

Fasten off, leaving a long yarn tail. Stuff the stem with fiberfill and insert floral wire, leaving the wire 2.5cm (1in) longer than the stem. Insert the stem into the center of the dirt. With a yarn needle and yarn tail, sew **Rnd 24** of the stem to the dirt.

PETALS (MAKE 9)

Rnd 1: with **white** yarn, sc 5 in magic ring [5]

Rnd 2: 2 sc in each st around [10]

Rnds 3–6: sc in each st around [10]

Rnd 7: (sc2tog) 5 times [5]

Sl st in next st. Fasten off, leaving a long yarn tail. Do not stuff with fiberfill stuffing. Flatten and sew opening closed with a yarn needle and yarn tail. Sew petals to the front loops from **Rnd 6** of the daisy. Bend the stem of the daisy so that the pot does not tip over.

LEAF (MAKE 2)

Rnd 1: with **green** yarn, ch 10, sl st in 2nd ch from hook, sc 1, hdc 1, dc 4, hdc 1, sc 3 in last ch, working on the other side of the foundation ch, hdc 1, dc 4, hdc 1, sc 1, sl st 1, sl st in beginning skipped ch st [20]

Invisible fasten off and weave in ends. Attach one leaf to either side of the stem.

Leaf Chart

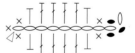

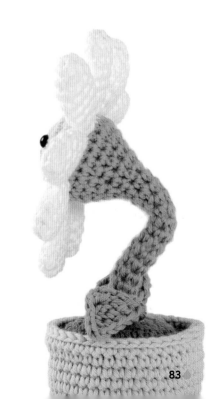

FORGET-ME-NOT

Materials

- 3.5mm (E/4) and 2.5mm (C/2) crochet hooks
- Paintbox Yarns Cotton Aran yarn: one 50g (1¾oz) ball each of Dolphin Blue (**dark blue**) and Soft Fudge (**brown**)
- Paintbox Yarns Cotton DK yarn: one 50g (1¾oz) ball each of Daffodil Yellow (**yellow**), Washed Teal (**light blue**), and Grass Green (**green**)
- Scraps of **black** and **pink** yarn
- 7mm safety eyes
- Fiberfill stuffing
- 20- and 26-gauge floral wire
- Yarn needle
- Stitch marker

Finished size

10cm (4in) tall by 7.5cm (3in) wide

Gauge

5 sc sts and 6 rows = 2.5cm (1in) using Aran yarn

6 sc sts and 7 rows = 2.5cm (1in) using DK yarn

POT

Rnd 1: with **3.5mm** hook and **dark blue Aran** yarn, sc 6 in magic ring [6]

Rnd 2: 2 sc in each st around [12]

Rnd 3: (sc 1, 2 sc in next st) 6 times [18]

Rnd 4: (sc 2, 2 sc in next st) 6 times [24]

Rnd 5: (sc 3, 2 sc in next st) 6 times [30]

Rnd 6: (sc 4, 2 sc in next st) 6 times [36]

Rnd 7: working in BLO, sc in each st around [36]

Rnds 8–11: sc in each st around [36]

Rnd 12: (sc 5, 2 sc in next st) 6 times [42]

Rnds 13–15: sc in each st around [42]

Place 7mm safety eyes between **Rnds 11 and 12**, with 4 sts in between. Begin to stuff with fiberfill. Do not finish off and cut yarn. Make the dirt before moving on to **Rnd 16**.

Rnd 16: place the dirt in the pot and line up the stitches from **Rnd 15** of the pot and **Rnd 7** of the dirt. With the yarn used to make the pot, sc in each st around, working in both loops of both pieces to join them together (see Making Up: Crocheting Two Pieces Together) [42]

Rnd 17: ch 1, sc in each st around, join with sl st in first st [42]

Rnd 18: sl st in each st around [42]

Invisible fasten off (see Finishing: Invisible Fasten Off) and weave in ends. Add stitches for the mouth and cheeks using **black** and **pink** yarn (see Making Up: Stitching Facial Details). Begin shaping by inserting needle from center bottom to center top, then take needle back down from center top to slightly off center bottom and back up to center top. Pull to create an indentation in the bottom of the pot. Fasten off and weave in ends.

DIRT

Rnd 1: with **3.5mm** hook and **brown Aran** yarn, sc 6 in magic ring [6]

Rnd 2: 2 sc in each st around [12]

Rnd 3: (sc 1, 2 sc in next st) 6 times [18]

Rnd 4: (sc 2, 2 sc in next st) 6 times [24]

Rnd 5: (sc 3, 2 sc in next st) 6 times [30]

Rnd 6: (sc 4, 2 sc in next st) 6 times [36]

Rnd 7: (sc 5, 2 sc in next st) 6 times [42]

Invisible fasten off and weave in ends.

FORGET-ME-NOT (MAKE 12)

Rnd 1: with **2.5mm** hook and **yellow DK** yarn, sc 5 in magic ring [5]

Rnd 2: change to **light blue DK** yarn, (sl st + ch 2 + 2 dc + ch 2 + sl st) 5 times [5 petals]

Fasten off and weave in ends.

Make 12 yarn-wrapped blossom stems (see Making Up: Yarn-Wrapped Blossom Stem). Attach each forget-me-not to a stem and insert into the pot (1).

LEAF (MAKE 12)

Rnd 1: cut a 10-cm (4-in) piece of 26-gauge floral wire. With **2.5mm** hook and **green DK** yarn, ch 6, hold wire behind the foundation ch and crochet the following sts around the wire (see Making Up: Crocheting with Floral Wire): sc in 2nd ch from hook, hdc 1, dc 1, hdc 1, 3 sc in last ch, working on the other side of the foundation ch, hdc 1, dc 1, hdc 1, sc 1, sl st in beginning skipped ch st [12]

Invisible fasten off and weave in all ends (2).

Insert the leaves into the pot.

NOT KIDDING...

Yarn balls are easier to work with. So, turn your skeins into balls to help prevent any unwanted yarn tangles or inconsistent tension in your work.

As early as the 15th century, purple dyes were produced from sea snails. One of the first synthetic dyes was also a shade of purple—it was created from chemicals derived from coal tar.

IRiS BULB

Materials

- 2.5mm (C/2) crochet hook
- Paintbox Yarns Cotton DK yarn: one 50g (1¾oz) ball each of Champagne White (**cream**), Light Caramel (**tan**), Grass Green (**green**), Pansy Purple (**purple**), and Daffodil Yellow (**yellow**)
- Scraps of **black** and **pink** yarn
- 6mm safety eyes
- Fiberfill stuffing
- Yarn needle
- Stitch marker

Finished size

15cm (6in) tall by 6.5cm (2½in) wide

Gauge

6 sc sts and 7 rows = 2.5cm (1in)

BULB

Rnd 1: with **cream** yarn, sc 6 in magic ring [6]

Rnd 2: 2 sc in each st around [12]

Rnd 3: change to **tan** yarn, (sc 1, 2 sc in next st) 6 times [18]

Rnd 4: (sc 2, 2 sc in next st) 6 times [24]

Rnd 5: (sc 3, 2 sc in next st) 6 times [30]

Rnd 6: (sc 4, 2 sc in next st) 6 times [36]

Rnd 7: (sc 5, 2 sc in next st) 6 times [42]

Rnd 8: (sc 6, 2 sc in next st) 6 times [48]

Rnds 9–13: sc in each st around [48]

Rnd 14: (sc 3, sc2tog, sc 3) 6 times [42]

Rnd 15: (sc2tog, sc 5) 6 times [36]

Rnd 16: (sc 2, sc2tog, sc 2) 6 times [30]

Place 6mm safety eyes between **Rnds 10 and 11**, with 5 sts in between. Begin to stuff with fiberfill.

Rnd 17: (sc2tog, sc 3) 6 times [24]

Rnd 18: sc in each st around [24]

Rnd 19: (sc 1, sc2tog, sc 1) 6 times [18]

Rnd 20: sc in each st around [18]

Rnd 21: (sc2tog, sc 1) 6 times [12]

Rnd 22: change to **green** yarn, working in BLO, sc in each st around [12]

Rnd 23: working in BLO, (sc2tog, sc 2) 3 times [9]

Rnds 24–27: sc in each st around [9]

Rnd 28: working in BLO, sc in each st around [9]

Rnd 29: working in BLO, (sc2tog, sc 1) 3 times [6]

Finish stuffing. Fasten off, leaving a long yarn tail. With a yarn needle, weave the tail through FLO to close the opening. Weave in all ends. Add stitches for the mouth and cheeks using **black** and **pink** yarn (see Making Up: Stitching Facial Details). Fasten off and weave in ends. Make and sew on three sizes of petals before moving on to **Rnd 30**.

Rnd 30: join **green** yarn in any front loop from **Rnd 23**, (ch 8, sl st in 2nd ch from hook, sc 1, hdc 5, sl st in next 2 sts from **Rnd 23**, ch 10, sl st in 2nd ch from hook, sc 1, hdc 7, sl st in next st from **Rnd 23**) 3 times [60]

Fasten off and weave in ends.

Rnd 31: join **tan** yarn in any front loop from **Rnd 22**, (sc 3, 2 sc in next st) 3 times [15]

Rnd 32: sc in each st around [15]

Fasten off and weave in ends. Tie short lengths of **cream** yarn to **Rnds 1 and 2**. Cut them all the same length and unravel yarn to make it fuzzy.

SMALL PETAL (MAKE 3)

Rnd 1: with **purple** yarn, ch 9, sc in 2nd ch from hook, sc 6, 2 dc + sc + 2 dc in last st, working on the other side of the foundation ch, sc 7 [19]

Fasten off, leaving a long yarn tail (1). Sew the small petals to the front loops that were created from weaving in the yarn tail at the end of **Rnd 29** (2).

MEDIUM PETAL (MAKE 3)

Rnd 1: with **purple** yarn, ch 9, sc in 2nd ch from hook, sc 2, 2 hdc in next 2 sts, 2 dc in next 2 sts, 3 tr in last st, working on the other side of the foundation ch, 2 dc in next 2 sts, 2 hdc in next 2 sts, sc 3 [25]

Rnd 2: sl st 3, (sc + ch 1) 9 times, hdc + dc + hdc in next st, (ch 1 + sc) 9 times, sl st 3 [45]

Fasten off, leaving a long yarn tail (1). Sew the medium petals to the front loops from **Rnd 29**.

LARGE PETAL (MAKE 3)

Rnd 1: with **yellow** yarn, ch 10, sc in 2nd ch from hook, sc 7, 2 sc in last st, change to **purple** yarn, working on the other side of the foundation ch, sc 1, hdc 1, dc 1, 2 dc in next 2 sts, 2 tr in next 2 sts, 3 tr in next st, working on the other side, 3 tr in next st, 2 tr in next 2 sts, 2 dc in next 2 sts, dc 1, hdc 1, sc 3 [40]

Rnd 2: sl st 4, (sc + ch 1) 10 times, hdc + dc + hdc in next st, (ch 1 + sc) 10 times, sl st 5 [52]

Fasten off, leaving a long yarn tail (1). Sew the large petals to the front loops from **Rnd 28**.

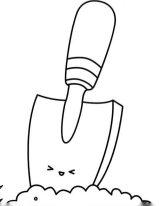

PANSY

Materials

- 3.5mm (E/4) and 2.5mm (C/2) crochet hooks
- Paintbox Yarns Cotton Aran yarn: one 50g (1¾oz) ball each of Tea Rose (**purple**) and Washed Teal (**blue**)
- Paintbox Yarns Cotton DK yarn: one 50g (1¾oz) ball each of Daffodil Yellow (**yellow**), Pansy Purple (**dark purple**), Paper White (**white**), and Grass Green (**green**)
- Scraps of **black** and **pink** yarn
- 7mm safety eyes
- Fiberfill stuffing
- 16-gauge floral wire
- Yarn needle
- Stitch marker

Finished size

16.5cm (6½in) tall by 9cm (3½in) wide

Gauge

5 sc sts and 6 rows = 2.5cm (1in) using Aran yarn

6 sc sts and 7 rows = 2.5cm (1in) using DK yarn

VASE

Rnd 1: with **3.5mm** hook and **purple Aran** yarn, sc 6 in magic ring [6]

Rnd 2: 2 sc in each st around [12]

Rnd 3: (sc 1, 2 sc in next st) 6 times [18]

Rnd 4: (sc 2, 2 sc in next st) 6 times [24]

Rnd 5: (sc 3, 2 sc in next st) 6 times [30]

Rnd 6: (sc 4, 2 sc in next st) 6 times [36]

Rnd 7: working in BLO, sc in each st around [36]

Rnd 8: sc in each st around [36]

Rnd 9: (sc 5, 2 sc in next st) 6 times [42]

Rnds 10–16: sc in each st around [42]

Rnd 17: (sc2tog, sc 5) 6 times [36]

Rnd 18: (sc 2, sc2tog, sc 2) 6 times [30]

Rnd 19: (sc2tog, sc 3) 6 times [24]

Place 7mm safety eyes between **Rnds 11 and 12**, with 4 sts in between. Stuff with fiberfill. Do not finish off and cut yarn. Make the water before moving on to **Rnd 20**.

Rnd 20: place the water in the vase and line up the stitches from **Rnd 19** of the vase and **Rnd 4** of the water. With the yarn used to make the vase, sc in each st around, working in both loops of both pieces to join them together (see Making Up: Crocheting Two Pieces Together) [24]

Rnds 21–22: sc in each st around [24]

Rnd 23: (sc 3, 2 sc in next st) 6 times [30]

Rnds 24–25: sc in each st around [30]

Rnd 26: sl st in each st around [30]

Invisible fasten off (see Finishing: Invisible Fasten Off) and weave in ends. Add stitches for the mouth and cheeks using **black** and pink yarn (see Making Up: Stitching Facial Details). Begin shaping by inserting needle from center bottom to center top, then take needle back down from center top to slightly off center bottom and back up to center top. Pull to create an indentation in the bottom of the vase. Fasten off and weave in ends.

WATER

Rnd 1: with **3.5mm** hook and **blue Aran** yarn, sc 6 in magic ring [6]

Rnd 2: 2 sc in each st around [12]

Rnd 3: (sc 1, 2 sc in next st) 6 times [18]

Rnd 4: (sc 2, 2 sc in next st) 6 times [24]

Invisible fasten off and weave in ends.

PANSY (MAKE 3)

Rnd 1: with **2.5mm** hook and **yellow DK** yarn, sc 12 in magic ring [12]

You will now make the 2 large purple petals at the back of the pansy, first working 2 rows back and forth before continuing to work in the round.

Row 2: change to **dark purple DK** yarn, working in BLO, sc 1, (ch 4, skip next st, sc 1) 2 times, leave remaining sts unworked, turn [11]

Row 3: ch 1, sc 1, (8 dc in next ch-4 space, sc in next sc st) 2 times, turn [19]

Return to working in the round.

Rnd 4: ch 1, sc 1, sc 1 + hdc 1 in next st, hdc 1 + dc 1 in next st, dc 1 + tr 1 in next st, 2 tr in next 5 sts, ch 3, sc 1, ch 3, 2 tr in next 5 sts, tr 1 + dc 1 in next st, dc 1 + hdc 1 in next st, hdc 1 + sc 1 in next st, sc 1 [41]

In **Rnd 5** you will be working in the front loop stitches from **Rnd 1**, beginning in the next unworked st.

Rnd 5: working in FLO, 2 dc in next st, sc 1, 2 dc in next st, 2 tr in next st, 2 dc in next st, sc 1, 2 dc in next st, 2 tr in next st, 2 dc in next st, sc 1, 2 dc in next st, 2 tr in next st, sl st in first dc st [22]

Fasten off and weave in ends.

Rnd 6: join **white DK** yarn in next sc st, ch 3, 2 tr in next 6 sts, ch 3, sl st in next sc st, (ch 3, 2 dc in next 2 sts, 2 tr in next 2 sts, 2 dc in next 2 sts, ch 3, sl st in next sc st) 2 times [57]

Fasten off and weave in ends.

Rnd 7: join **green DK** yarn in any back loop from **Rnd 1**, working in BLO including the 3 back loops that have already been worked in, sc in each st around [12]

Rnd 8: sc in each st around [12]

Rnd 9: (sc2tog, sc 2) 3 times [9]

Rnd 10: sc in each st around [9]

Begin to stuff with fiberfill.

Rnd 11: (sc2tog, sc 1) 3 times [6]

Rnds 12–20: sc in each st around [6]

Sl st in next st, finish stuffing with fiberfill, insert floral wire into stem leaving 2.5cm (1in) extending past the stem. Fasten off and weave in ends. Bend the head of the pansy slightly forward.

LEAF (MAKE 9)

Rnd 1: with **2.5mm** hook and **green DK** yarn, ch 10, sl st in 2nd ch from hook, sc 1, hdc 1, dc 4, hdc 1, sc 3 in last ch, working on the other side of the foundation ch, hdc 1, dc 4, hdc 1, sc 1, sl st 1, sl st in beginning skipped ch st [20]

Invisible fasten off and weave in ends.

Attach three leaves to each pansy stem (1).

Insert the pansies into the vase (2).

1

2

Leaf Chart

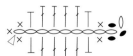

AFRICAN VIOLET

Materials

- 3.5mm (E/4) and 2.5mm (C/2) crochet hooks
- Paintbox Yarns Cotton Aran yarn: one 50g (1¾oz) ball each of Vanilla Cream (**cream**), Soft Fudge (**brown**) and Racing Green (**dark green**)
- Paintbox Yarns Cotton DK yarn: one 50g (1¾oz) ball each of Daffodil Yellow (**yellow**) and Pansy Purple (**purple**)
- Scraps of **black** and **pink** yarn
- 7mm safety eyes
- Fiberfill stuffing
- Yarn needle
- Stitch marker

Finished size

10cm (4in) tall by 7.5cm (3in) wide

Gauge

5 sc sts and 6 rows = 2.5cm (1in) using Aran yarn

6 sc sts and 7 rows = 2.5cm (1in) using DK yarn

DIRT

Rnd 1: with **3.5mm** hook and **brown Aran** yarn, sc 6 in magic ring [6]

Rnd 2: 2 sc in each st around [12]

Rnd 3: (sc 1, 2 sc in next st) 6 times [18]

Rnd 4: (sc 2, 2 sc in next st) 6 times [24]

Rnd 5: (sc 3, 2 sc in next st) 6 times [30]

Rnd 6: (sc 4, 2 sc in next st) 6 times [36]

Rnd 7: (sc 5, 2 sc in next st) 6 times [42]

Invisible fasten off and weave in ends.

POT

Rnd 1: with **3.5mm** hook and **cream Aran** yarn, sc 6 in magic ring [6]

Rnd 2: 2 sc in each st around [12]

Rnd 3: (sc 1, 2 sc in next st) 6 times [18]

Rnd 4: (sc 2, 2 sc in next st) 6 times [24]

Rnd 5: (sc 3, 2 sc in next st) 6 times [30]

Rnd 6: (sc 4, 2 sc in next st) 6 times [36]

Rnd 7: working in BLO, sc in each st around [36]

Rnds 8–11: sc in each st around [36]

Rnd 12: (sc 5, 2 sc in next st) 6 times [42]

Rnds 13–15: sc in each st around [42]

Place 7mm safety eyes between **Rnds 11 and 12**, with 4 sts in between. Begin to stuff with fiberfill. Do not finish off and cut yarn.

1

2

Make the dirt before moving on to **Rnd 16**.

Rnd 16: place the dirt in the pot and line up the stitches from **Rnd 15** of the pot and **Rnd 7** of the dirt. With the yarn used to make the pot, sc in each st around, working in both loops of both pieces to join them together (see Making Up: Crocheting Two Pieces Together) [42]

Rnd 17: ch 1, sc in each st around, join with sl st in first st [42]

Rnd 18: sl st in each st around [42]

Invisible fasten off (see Finishing: Invisible Fasten Off) and weave in ends. Add stitches for the mouth, eyelashes, and cheeks using **black** and **pink** yarn (see Making Up: Stitching Facial Details). Begin shaping by inserting needle from center bottom to center top, then take needle back down from center top to slightly off center bottom and back up to center top. Pull to create an indentation in the bottom of the pot. Fasten off and weave in ends (1).

LEAF (MAKE 8)

Rnd 1: with **3.5mm** hook and **dark green Aran** yarn, sc 6 in magic ring [6]

Rnd 2: 2 sc in each st around [12]

Rnd 3: sc 2, 2 sc in next 2 sts, 2 hdc in next 2 sts, ch 1, 2 hdc in next 2 sts, 2 sc in next 2 sts, sc 2 [21]

Rnd 4: sl st in each st around [21]

Invisible fasten off and weave in all ends. Attach the leaves to the dirt (2).

VIOLET (MAKE 6)

Rnd 1: with **2.5mm** hook and **yellow DK** yarn, sc 5 in magic ring [5]

Rnd 2: change to **purple** yarn, (sl st + ch 3 + 3 dc + ch 3 + sl st) 5 times [5 petals]

Finish off and weave in ends. Attach the violets to the leaves.

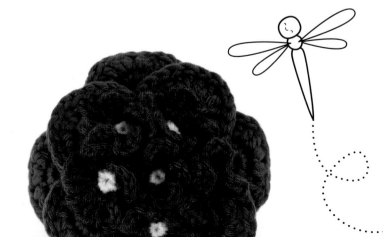

RANUNCULUS

Materials

- 3.5mm (E/4) and 2.5mm (C/2) crochet hooks
- Paintbox Yarns Cotton Aran yarn: one 50g (1¾oz) ball each of Dusty Lilac (**purple**) and Soft Fudge (**brown**)
- Paintbox Yarns Cotton DK yarn: one 50g (1¾oz) ball each of Lime Green (**lime green**) and Tea Rose (**lilac**)
- Scraps of **black** and **pink** yarn
- 7mm safety eyes
- Fiberfill stuffing
- Yarn needle
- Stitch marker

Finished size

10cm (4in) tall by 7.5cm (3in) wide

Gauge

5 sc sts and 6 rows = 2.5cm (1in) using Aran yarn

6 sc sts and 7 rows = 2.5cm (1in) using DK yarn

POT

Rnd 1: with **3.5mm** hook and **purple Aran** yarn, sc 6 in magic ring [6]

Rnd 2: 2 sc in each st around [12]

Rnd 3: (sc 1, 2 sc in next st) 6 times [18]

Rnd 4: (sc 2, 2 sc in next st) 6 times [24]

Rnd 5: (sc 3, 2 sc in next st) 6 times [30]

Rnd 6: (sc 4, 2 sc in next st) 6 times [36]

Rnd 7: working in BLO, sc in each st around [36]

Rnds 8–11: sc in each st around [36]

Rnd 12: (sc 5, 2 sc in next st) 6 times [42]

Rnds 13–15: sc in each st around [42]

Place 7mm safety eyes between **Rnds 11 and 12**, with 4 sts in between. Begin to stuff with fiberfill. Do not finish off and cut yarn. Make the dirt before moving on to **Rnd 16.**

Rnd 16: place the dirt in the pot and line up the stitches from **Rnd 15** of the pot and **Rnd 7** of the dirt. With the yarn used to make the pot, sc in each st around, working in both loops of both pieces to join them together (see Making Up: Crocheting Two Pieces Together) [42]

Rnd 17: ch 1, sc in each st around, join with sl st in first st [42]

Rnd 18: sl st in each st around [42]

Invisible fasten off (see Finishing: Invisible Fasten Off) and weave in ends. Add stitches for the mouth and cheeks using **black** and **pink** yarn (see Making Up: Stitching Facial Details). Begin shaping by inserting needle from center bottom to center top, then take needle back down from center top to slightly off center bottom and back up to center top. Pull to create an indentation in the bottom of the pot. Fasten off and weave in ends.

DIRT

Rnd 1: with **3.5mm** hook and **brown Aran** yarn, sc 6 in magic ring [6]

Rnd 2: 2 sc in each st around [12]

Rnd 3: (sc 1, 2 sc in next st) 6 times [18]

Rnd 4: (sc 2, 2 sc in next st) 6 times [24]

Rnd 5: (sc 3, 2 sc in next st) 6 times [30]

Rnd 6: (sc 4, 2 sc in next st) 6 times [36]

Rnd 7: (sc 5, 2 sc in next st) 6 times [42]

Invisible fasten off and weave in ends.

INNER LAYER

Rnd 1: with **2.5mm** hook and **lime green DK** yarn, sc 10 in magic ring [10]

Row 2: skip next st, 4 sc in next st, turn [4]

Row 3: ch 1 (does not count as a st), sc 1, 2 sc in next 2 sts, sc 1, turn [6]

Rows 4–5: ch 1, sc in each st across, turn [6]

Row 6: ch 1, sc2tog, sc 2, sc2tog, do NOT turn [4]

Row 7: sl st down the side of the petal [6]

Repeat **Rows 2–7** five times for a total of five petals. Fasten off and weave in ends.

SECOND LAYER

Rnd 1: with **2.5mm** hook and **lilac DK** yarn, sc 10 in magic ring [10]

Row 2: skip next st, 4 sc in next st, turn [4]

Row 3: ch 1, sc 1, 2 sc in next 2 sts, sc 1, turn [6]

Row 4: ch 1, sc 1, 2 sc in next 4 sts, sc 1, turn [10]

Rows 5–7: ch 1, sc in each st across, turn [10]

Row 8: ch 1, sc2tog, sc 6, sc2tog, do NOT turn [8]

Row 9: sl st down the side of the petal [8]

Repeat **Rows 2–9** four more times for a total of five petals. Fasten off and weave in ends.

THIRD LAYER

Rnd 1: with **2.5mm** hook and **lilac DK** yarn, sc 10 in magic ring [10]

Row 2: skip next st, 4 sc in next st, turn [4]

Row 3: ch 1, sc 1, 2 sc in next 2 sts, sc 1, turn [6]

Row 4: ch 1, sc 1, 2 sc in next 4 sts, sc 1, turn [10]

Row 5: ch 1, sc 4, 2 sc in next 2 sts, sc 4, turn [12]

Rows 6–9: ch 1, sc in each st across, turn [12]

Row 10: ch 1, sc2tog, sc 8, sc2tog, do NOT turn [10]

Row 11: sl st down the side of the petal [10]

Repeat **Rows 2–11** four more times for a total of five petals. Fasten off and weave in ends.

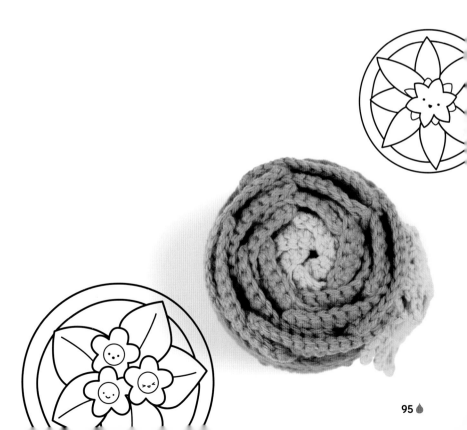

FOURTH LAYER

Rnd 1: with **2.5mm** hook and **lilac DK** yarn, sc 10 in magic ring [10]

Row 2: skip next st, 4 sc in next st, turn [4]

Row 3: ch 1, sc 1, 2 sc in next 2 sts, sc 1, turn [6]

Row 4: ch 1, sc 1, 2 sc in next 4 sts, sc 1, turn [10]

Row 5: ch 1, sc 3, 2 sc in next 4 sts, sc 3, turn [14]

Rows 6–11: ch 1, sc in each st across, turn [14]

Row 12: ch 1, sc2tog, sc 10, sc2tog, do NOT turn [12]

Row 13: sl st down the side of the petal [12]

Repeat **Rows 2–13** four more times for a total of five petals. Fasten off and weave in ends.

Starting with the inner layer, overlap the petals to form a closed shape. Apply a bit of glue in between each petal until they are all glued together. Apply a bit of glue to the bottom of the inner layer and place it in the middle of the second layer. Overlap the petals of the second layer and glue the overlapping parts of the petals together (1).

Repeat for the third and fourth layers (2).

Attach the flower to the dirt.

LEAF (MAKE 2)

Rnd 1: with **2.5mm** hook and **lime green DK** yarn, ch 10, sc in 2nd ch from hook, sc 8, ch 2, working on the other side of the foundation ch, sc 1, (ch 4, sc in 2nd ch from hook, sc in next 2 ch sts, sc 2) 4 times [32]

Rnd 2: (ch 4, sc in 2nd ch from hook, sc in next 2 ch sts, sc 2) 5 times [25]

Invisible fasten off and weave in all ends (2). Attach the leaves to the dirt.

Leaf Chart

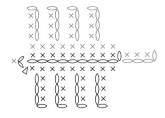

1

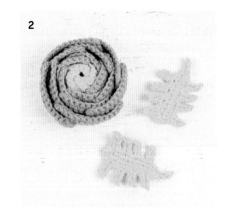

2

BEETLE

Materials

- 2.5mm (C/2) crochet hook
- Paintbox Yarns Cotton DK yarn: one 50g (1¾oz) ball each of Pansy Purple (**purple**) and Pure Black (**black**)
- 6mm safety eyes
- Fiberfill stuffing
- Yarn needle
- Stitch marker

Finished size

2.5cm (1in) tall by 7.5cm (3in) wide

Gauge

6 sc sts and 7 rows = 2.5cm (1in)

TOP PIECE

Rnd 1: with **purple** yarn, ch 9, 3 sc in 2nd ch from hook, sc 6, 3 sc in last ch, working on the other side of the foundation ch, sc 6, skip last st [18]

Rnd 2: (2 sc in next 3 sts, sc 6) 2 times [24]

Rnd 3: (sc 1, 2 sc in next st) 3 times, sc 6, (sc 1, 2 sc in next st) 3 times, sc 6 [30]

Rnds 4–6: sc in each st around [30]

Fasten off and weave in ends. With a yarn needle and using **black** yarn, stitch a line lengthwise down the center.

BOTTOM PIECE

With **black** yarn, ch 9

Rnd 1: 3 sc in 2nd ch from hook, sc 6, 3 sc in last ch, working on the other side of the foundation ch, sc 6, skip last st [18]

Rnd 2: (2 sc in next 3 sts, sc 6) 2 times [24]

Rnd 3: (sc 1, 2 sc in next st) 3 times, sc 6, (sc 1, 2 sc in next st) 3 times, sc 6 [30], sc 5 to begin a new starting point for the next rnd. Begin to stuff with fiberfill.

Rnd 4: place the top piece under the bottom piece and line up the stitches from **Rnd 6** of the top piece and **Rnd 3** of the bottom piece. With the yarn used to make the bottom piece and working in BLO of both pieces to join them together, continue stuffing as you go, *sl st 3, (sl st + ch 8 + sl st in 2nd ch from hook + sl st in next 6 ch sts + sl st), repeat from * 2 times, sl st 3, **sl st 3, (sl st + ch 8 + sl st in 2nd ch from hook + sl st in next 6 ch sts + sl st), repeat from ** 2 times, sl st 3 [78]

Fasten off and weave in ends.

ANTENNA (MAKE 2)

Rnd 1: with **black** yarn, ch 6, working in back bump loops, sc in 2nd ch from hook, sl st in next 4 ch sts [5]

Fasten off and do not weave in ends.

HEAD

Rnd 1: with **purple** yarn, sc 5 in magic ring [5]

Rnd 2: 2 sc in each st around [10]

Rnd 3: (sc 1, 2 sc in next st) 5 times [15]

Rnds 4–5: sc in each st around [15]

Place 6mm safety eyes between **Rnds 2 and 3**, with 4 sts in between. Attach antennae between **Rnds 4 and 5**, directly above the eyes. Begin to stuff with fiberfill.

Rnd 6: working in BLO, (sc 1, sc2tog) 5 times [10]

Rnd 7: (sc2tog) 5 times [5]

Finish stuffing. Fasten off, leaving a long yarn tail. With a yarn needle, weave the tail through FLO to close the opening. Weave in all ends. Attach the head to the front of the body.

White is not technically a color, but
rather the wavelengths of all the colors
combined. We could not see all the beautiful
colors in nature if it wasn't for white
light—so white literally lights the way.

PAPERWHITE BULB

Materials

- 2.5mm (C/2) crochet hook
- Paintbox Yarns Cotton DK yarn: one 50g (1¾oz) ball each of Champagne White (**cream**), Light Caramel (**tan**), Grass Green (**green**), and Paper White (**white**)
- Scraps of **black** and **pink** yarn
- 6mm safety eyes
- Fiberfill stuffing
- Yarn needle
- Stitch marker

Finished size

15cm (6in) tall by 6.5cm (2½in) wide

Gauge

6 sc sts and 7 rows = 2.5cm (1in)

BULB

Rnd 1: with **cream** yarn, sc 6 in magic ring [6]

Rnd 2: 2 sc in each st around [12]

Rnd 3: change to **tan** yarn, (sc 1, 2 sc in next st) 6 times [18]

Rnd 4: (sc 2, 2 sc in next st) 6 times [24]

Rnd 5: (sc 3, 2 sc in next st) 6 times [30]

Rnd 6: (sc 4, 2 sc in next st) 6 times [36]

Rnd 7: (sc 5, 2 sc in next st) 6 times [42]

Rnd 8: (sc 6, 2 sc in next st) 6 times [48]

Rnds 9–13: sc in each st around [48]

Rnd 14: (sc 3, sc2tog, sc 3) 6 times [42]

Rnd 15: (sc2tog, sc 5) 6 times [36]

Rnd 16: (sc 2, sc2tog, sc 2) 6 times [30]

Place 6mm safety eyes between **Rnds 10 and 11**, with 5 sts in between. Begin to stuff with fiberfill.

Rnd 17: (sc2tog, sc 3) 6 times [24]

Rnd 18: sc in each st around [24]

Rnd 19: (sc 1, sc2tog, sc 1) 6 times [18]

Rnd 20: sc in each st around [18]

Rnd 21: (sc2tog, sc 1) 6 times [12]

Rnd 22: change to **green** yarn, working in BLO, sc in each st around [12]

Rnd 23: working in BLO, (sc2tog, sc 2) 3 times [9]

Rnds 24–25: sc in each st around [9]

Rnd 26: (sc2tog, sc 1) 3 times [6]

Rnds 27-28: sc in each st around [6]

Finish stuffing. Fasten off, leaving a long yarn tail. With a yarn needle, weave the tail through BLO to close the opening. Weave in all ends. Add stitches for the mouth and cheeks using **black** and **pink** yarn (see Making Up: Stitching Facial Details).

Rnd 29: join **green** yarn in any front loop from **Rnd 28**, (sl st 1, ch 6, sl st in 2nd ch from hook, sl st 4, sl st in next st from **Rnd 28**) 3 times [21]

Fasten off and weave in ends.

Rnd 30: join **green** yarn in any front loop from **Rnd 23**, (sl st, ch 8, sl st in 2nd ch from hook, sl st 6, sl st in next st from **Rnd 23**, ch 6, sl st in 2nd ch from hook, sl st 4, sl st in next 2 sts from **Rnd 23**) 3 times [45]

Rnd 31: join **tan** yarn in any front loop from **Rnd 22**, sc in each st around [12]

Rnd 32: sc in each st around [12]

Fasten off and weave in ends. Tie short lengths of **cream** yarn to **Rnds 1 and 2**. Cut them all the same length and unravel yarn to make it fuzzy.

FLOWER (MAKE 3)

Rnd 1: with **white** yarn, sc 5 in magic ring [5]

Rnd 2: (sl st + ch 2 + dc + ch 2 + sl st) 5 times [5 petals]

Fasten off and weave in ends. Attach the flowers to the top of the bulb.

UNBE-LEAF-ABLY FUNNY...

Why do gardeners plant bulbs? So the worms can see where they're going!

LiLY OF THE VALLEY

Materials

- 3.5mm (E/4) and 2.5mm (C/2) crochet hooks
- Paintbox Yarns Cotton Aran yarn: one 50g (1¾oz) ball each of Paper White (**white**), Washed Teal (**blue**), and Grass Green (**green**)
- Paintbox Yarns Cotton DK yarn: one 50g (1¾oz) ball of Paper White (**white**)
- Scraps of **black** and **pink** yarn
- 7mm safety eyes
- Fiberfill stuffing
- 26-gauge floral wire
- Yarn needle
- Stitch marker

Finished size

16.5cm (6½in) tall by 7.5cm (3in) wide

Gauge

5 sc sts and 6 rows = 2.5cm (1in) using Aran yarn

6 sc sts and 7 rows = 2.5cm (1in) using DK yarn

VASE

Rnd 1: with **3.5mm** hook and **white Aran** yarn, sc 6 in magic ring [6]

Rnd 2: 2 sc in each st around [12]

Rnd 3: (sc 1, 2 sc in next st) 6 times [18]

Rnd 4: (sc 2, 2 sc in next st) 6 times [24]

Rnd 5: (sc 3, 2 sc in next st) 6 times [30]

Rnd 6: (sc 4, 2 sc in next st) 6 times [36]

Rnd 7: working in BLO, sc in each st around [36]

Rnd 8: sc in each st around [36]

Rnd 9: (sc 5, 2 sc in next st) 6 times [42]

Rnds 10–16: sc in each st around [42]

Rnd 17: (sc2tog, sc 5) 6 times [36]

Rnd 18: (sc 2, sc2tog, sc 2) 6 times [30]

Rnd 19: (sc2tog, sc 3) 6 times [24]

Place 7mm safety eyes between **Rnds 11 and 12**, with 4 sts in between. Stuff with fiberfill. Do not finish off and cut yarn. Make the water before moving on to **Rnd 20**.

Rnd 20: place the water in the vase and line up the stitches from **Rnd 19** of the vase and **Rnd 4** of the water. With the yarn used to make the vase, sc in each st around, working in both loops of both pieces to join them together (see Making Up: Crocheting Two Pieces Together) [24]

Rnds 21–22: sc in each st around [24]

Rnd 23: (sc 3, 2 sc in next st) 6 times [30]

Rnds 24–25: sc in each st around [30]

Rnd 26: sl st in each st around [30]

Invisible fasten off (see Finishing: Invisible Fasten Off) and weave in ends. Add stitches for the mouth and cheeks using **black** and **pink** yarn (see Making Up: Stitching Facial Details). Begin shaping by inserting needle from center bottom to center top, then take needle back down from center top to slightly off center bottom and back up to center top. Pull to create an indentation in the bottom of the vase. Fasten off and weave in ends.

WATER

Rnd 1: with **3.5mm** hook and **blue Aran** yarn, sc 6 in magic ring [6]

Rnd 2: 2 sc in each st around [12]

Rnd 3: (sc 1, 2 sc in next st) 6 times [18]

Rnd 4: (sc 2, 2 sc in next st) 6 times [24]

Invisible fasten off and weave in ends.

LEAF (MAKE 4)

Rnd 1: cut a 10-cm (4-in) piece of floral wire. With **3.5mm** hook and **green Aran** yarn, ch 15, hold wire behind the foundation ch, and crochet the following sts around the wire (see Making Up: Crocheting with Floral Wire): sc in 2nd ch from hook, sc 3, hdc 1, dc 6, hdc 1, sc 2, ch 6, sl st in 2nd ch from hook, sl st 4, working on the other side of the foundation ch, sc 2, hdc 1, dc 6, hdc 1, sc 4, sl st in first skipped st [34]

Fasten off and weave in ends. Bend the wire end behind sts at the top of the leaf, leaving the wire 2.5cm (1in) longer than the leaf stem (1).

FLOWER (MAKE 9)

Rnd 1: with **2.5mm** hook and **white DK** yarn, sc 4 in magic ring [4]

Rnd 2: 2 sc in each st around [8]

Rnds 3–4: sc in each st around [8]

Rnd 5: (2 dc in next st, sl st 1) 4 times [12]

Fasten off and weave in ends.

STEM (MAKE 3)

Rnd 1: cut a 10-cm (4-in) piece of floral wire. With **3.5mm** hook and **green Aran** yarn, ch 21, hold wire behind the foundation ch, and crochet the following sts around the wire: sl st in 2nd ch from hook, sl st 11, (ch 3, sl st in 2nd ch from hook, sl st 1, sl st in next 4 sts of foundation ch) 2 times [24]

Fasten off and weave in ends. Bend the wire end behind the sts, leaving the wire 2.5cm (1in) longer than the stem (1). Attach three flowers to each stem. Insert the leaves and flower stems into the vase.

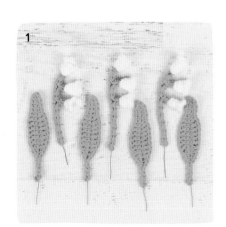

Leaf Chart

MOTH

Materials

- 2.5mm (C/2) crochet hook
- Paintbox Yarns Cotton DK yarn: one 50g (1¾oz) ball each of Pure Black (**black**), Champagne White (**cream**), and Paper White (**white**)
- 5mm safety eyes
- Fiberfill stuffing
- Yarn needle
- Stitch marker

Finished size

10cm (4in) tall by 9cm (3½in) wide

Gauge

6 sc sts and 7 rows = 2.5cm (1in)

ANTENNA (MAKE 2)

Rnd 1: with **black** yarn, ch 6, working in back bump loops, sc in 2nd ch from hook, sl st in next 4 ch sts [5]

Fasten off and do not weave in ends.

BODY

Rnd 1: with **cream** yarn, sc 6 in magic ring [6]

Rnd 2: 2 sc in each st around [12]

Rnd 3: (sc 1, 2 sc in next st) 6 times [18]

Rnds 4–6: sc in each st around [18]

Rnd 7: (sc2tog, sc 1) 6 times [12]

Rnd 8: (sc2tog, sc 4) 2 times [10]

Rnds 9–17: sc in each st around [10]

Place 5mm safety eyes between **Rnds 4 and 5**, with 3 sts in between. Attach antennae to **Rnd 2**, directly above the eyes. Begin to stuff with fiberfill.

Rnd 18: (sc2tog, sc 3) 2 times [8]

Rnd 19: sc in each st around [8]

Rnd 20: (sc2tog, sc 2) 2 times [6]

Finish stuffing. Fasten off, leaving a long yarn tail. With a yarn needle, weave the tail through FLO to close the opening. Weave in all ends (1).

SMALL WING (MAKE 2)

Rnd 1: with **cream** yarn, sc 5 in magic ring [5]

Rnd 2: 2 sc in each st around [10]

Rnd 3: (sc 1, 2 sc in next st) 5 times [15]

Rnd 4: (sc 1, 2 sc in next st) 2 times, 2 hdc in next st, 2 dc in next st, 2 tr in next st, 2 dc in next st, 2 hdc in next st, (2 sc in next st, sc 1) 2 times, sc 2 [24]

Invisible fasten off (see Finishing: Invisible Fasten Off) and weave in ends. Repeat **Rnds 1–4** to make a second small wing. Place one small wing on top of another, with right sides facing out. Insert hook through stitches of both pieces to join them together in the next rnd.

Rnd 5: with **white** yarn, sl st in each st around [24].

Invisible fasten off and weave in ends (1).

LARGE WING (MAKE 2)

Rnd 1: with **cream** yarn, sc 5 in magic ring [5]

Rnd 2: 2 sc in each st around [10]

Rnd 3: (sc 1, 2 sc in next st) 5 times [15]

Rnd 4: (sc 1, 2 sc in next st) 2 times, 2 hdc in next st, 2 dc in next st, 2 tr in next st, 2 dc in next st, 2 hdc in next st, (2 sc in next st, sc 1) 2 times, sc 2 [24]

Rnd 5: (sc 3, 2 sc in next st) 2 times, 2 hdc in next 6 sts, (2 sc in next st, sc 3) 2 times, sc 2 [34]

Invisible fasten off and weave in ends. Repeat **Rnds 1–5** to make a second large wing. Place one large wing on top of another, with right sides facing out. Insert hook through stitches of both pieces to join them together in the next rnd.

Rnd 6: with **white** yarn, sl st in each st around [34]

Invisible fasten off and weave in ends (1).

Attach both sets of large and small wings to the back of the moth's body with the large wings slightly overlapping the small wings (2).

JUST WING IT...

Instead of a moth, make a colorful butterfly by simply changing the yarn colors. Using your favorite colors will be sure to make your heart flutter!

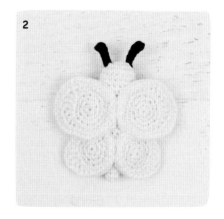

STRING OF PEARLS

Materials

- 3.5mm (E/4) and 2.5mm (C/2) crochet hooks
- Paintbox Yarns Cotton Aran yarn: one 50g (1¾oz) ball each of Vanilla Cream (**cream**), Paper White (**white**), and Soft Fudge (**brown**)
- Paintbox Yarns Cotton DK yarn: one 50g (1¾oz) ball of Pistachio Green (**pale green**)
- Scraps of **black** and **pink** yarn
- 8mm safety eyes
- Fiberfill stuffing
- Yarn needle
- Stitch marker

Finished size

10cm (4in) tall by 7.5cm (3in) wide

Gauge

5 sc sts and 6 rows = 2.5cm (1in) using Aran yarn

6 sc sts and 7 rows = 2.5cm (1in) using DK yarn

POT

Rnd 1: with **3.5mm** hook and **cream Aran** yarn, sc 6 in magic ring [6]

Rnd 2: 2 sc in each st around [12]

Rnd 3: (sc 1, 2 sc in next st) 6 times [18]

Rnd 4: (sc 2, 2 sc in next st) 6 times [24]

Rnd 5: (sc 3, 2 sc in next st) 6 times [30]

Rnd 6: (sc 4, 2 sc in next st) 6 times [36]

Rnd 7: working in BLO, sc in each st around [36]

Rnds 8–10: sc in each st around [36]

Rnd 11: change to **white Aran** yarn, sc in each st around [36]

Rnd 12: sc in each st around [36]

Rnd 13: (sc 5, 2 sc in next st) 6 times [42]

Rnds 14–19: sc in each st around [42]

Place 8mm safety eyes between **Rnds 14 and 15**, with 5 sts in between. Begin to stuff with fiberfill. Do not finish off and cut yarn. Make the dirt before moving on to **Rnd 20**.

Rnd 20: place the dirt in the pot and line up the stitches from **Rnd 19** of the pot and **Rnd 7** of the dirt. With the yarn used to make the pot, sc in each st around, working in both loops of both pieces to join them together (see Making Up: Crocheting Two Pieces Together) [42]

Rnd 21: ch 1, sc in each st around, join with sl st in first st [42]

Rnd 22: sl st in each st around [42]

Invisible fasten off (see Finishing: Invisible Fasten Off) and weave in ends. Add stitches for the mouth and cheeks using **black** and **pink** yarn (see Making Up: Stitching Facial Details). Begin shaping by inserting needle from center bottom to center top, then take needle back down from center top to slightly off center bottom and back up to center top. Pull to create an indentation in the bottom of the pot. Fasten off and weave in ends.

DIRT

Rnd 1: with **3.5mm** hook and **brown Aran** yarn, sc 6 in magic ring [6]

Rnd 2: 2 sc in each st around [12]

Rnd 3: (sc 1, 2 sc in next st) 6 times [18]

Rnd 4: (sc 2, 2 sc in next st) 6 times [24]

Rnd 5: (sc 3, 2 sc in next st) 6 times [30]

Rnd 6: (sc 4, 2 sc in next st) 6 times [36]

Rnd 7: (sc 5, 2 sc in next st) 6 times [42]

Invisible fasten off and weave in ends.

STRING OF PEARLS—LONG (MAKE 3)

Rnd 1: with **2.5mm** hook and **pale green DK** yarn, make a slip knot leaving a long yarn tail for sewing string of pearls to dirt, (ch 6, 5 dc in 2nd ch from hook, pull out hook and leave a big loop (1), place hook through the first dc st and the loop (2), tighten loop and pull through the first dc st) 9 times (3)

Fasten off and weave in end.

STRING OF PEARLS—MEDIUM (MAKE 6)

Rnd 1: with **2.5mm** hook and **pale green DK** yarn, make a slip knot leaving a long yarn tail for sewing string of pearls to dirt, (ch 6, 5 dc in 2nd ch from hook, pull out hook and leave a big loop, place hook through the first dc st and the loop, tighten loop and pull through the first dc st) 6 times

Fasten off and weave in end.

STRING OF PEARLS—SHORT (MAKE 9)

Rnd 1: with **2.5mm** hook and **pale green DK** yarn, make a slip knot leaving a long yarn tail for sewing string of pearls to dirt, (ch 6, 5 dc in 2nd ch from hook, pull out hook and leave a big loop, place hook through the first dc st and the loop, tighten loop and pull through the first dc st) 3 times

Fasten off and weave in end (4).

Sew all the strings of pearls to the top of the dirt.

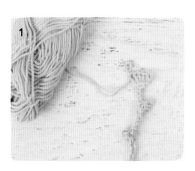
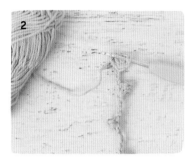
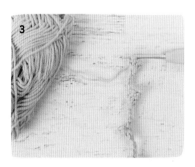
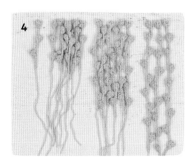

WATER LILY

Materials

- 3.5mm (E/4) and 2.5mm (C/2) crochet hooks
- Paintbox Yarns Cotton Aran yarn: one 50g (1¾oz) ball each of Paper White (**white**) and Washed Teal (**blue**)
- Paintbox Yarns Cotton DK yarn: one 50g (1¾oz) ball each of Spearmint Green (**green)**, Daffodil Yellow (**yellow**), and Paper White (**white**)
- Scraps of **black** and **pink** yarn
- 8mm safety eyes
- Fiberfill stuffing
- Yarn needle
- Stitch marker

Finished size

7.5cm (3in) tall by 12.5cm (5in) wide

Gauge

5 sc sts and 6 rows = 2.5cm (1in) using Aran yarn

6 sc sts and 7 rows = 2.5cm (1in) using DK yarn

POT

Rnd 1: with **3.5mm** hook and **white Aran** yarn, sc 6 in magic ring [6]

Rnd 2: 2 sc in each st around [12]

Rnd 3: (sc 1, 2 sc in next st) 6 times [18]

Rnd 4: (sc 2, 2 sc in next st) 6 times [24]

Rnd 5: (sc 3, 2 sc in next st) 6 times [30]

Rnd 6: (sc 4, 2 sc in next st) 6 times [36]

Rnd 7: (sc 5, 2 sc in next st) 6 times [42]

Rnd 8: (sc 6, 2 sc in next st) 6 times [48]

Rnd 9: (sc 7, 2 sc in next st) 6 times [54]

Rnd 10: (sc 8, 2 sc in next st) 6 times [60]

Rnd 11: working in BLO, sc in each st around [60]

Rnds 12–15: sc in each st around [60]

Rnd 16: (sc 9, 2 sc in next st) repeat 6 times [66]

Rnds 17–18: sc in each st around [66]

Place 8mm safety eyes between **Rnds 15 and 16**, with 5 sts in between. Begin to stuff with fiberfill. Do not finish off and cut yarn. Make the water before moving on to **Rnd 19**.

Rnd 19: place the water in the pot and line up the stitches from **Rnd 18** of the pot and **Rnd 11** of the water. With the yarn used to make the pot, sc in each st around, working in both loops of both pieces to join them together (see Making Up; Crocheting Two Pieces Together) [66]

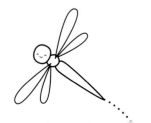

Rnd 20: ch 1, sc in each st around, join with sl st in first st [66]

Rnd 21: sl st in each st around [66]

Invisible fasten off (see Finishing: Invisible Fasten Off) and weave in ends. Add stitches for the mouth and cheeks using **black** and **pink** yarn (see Making Up: Stitching Facial Details). Begin shaping by inserting needle from center bottom to center top, then take needle back down from center top to slightly off center bottom and back up to center top. Pull to create an indentation in the bottom of the pot. Fasten off and weave in ends.

WATER

Rnd 1: with **3.5mm** hook and **blue Aran** yarn, sc 6 in magic ring [6]

Rnd 2: 2 sc in each st around [12]

Rnd 3: (sc 1, 2 sc in next st) 6 times [18]

Rnd 4: (sc 2, 2 sc in next st) 6 times [24]

Rnd 5: (sc 3, 2 sc in next st) 6 times [30]

Rnd 6: (sc 4, 2 sc in next st) 6 times [36]

Rnd 7: (sc 5, 2 sc in next st) 6 times [42]

Rnd 8: (sc 6, 2 sc in next st) 6 times [48]

Rnd 9: (sc 7, 2 sc in next st) 6 times [54]

Rnd 10: (sc 8, 2 sc in next st) 6 times [60]

Rnd 11: (sc 9, 2 sc in next st) 6 times [66]

Invisible fasten off and weave in ends.

LILYPAD

Rnd 1: with **2.5mm** hook and **green DK** yarn, sc 6 in magic ring [6]

Rnd 2: 2 sc in each st around [12]

Rnd 3: (sc 1, 2 sc in next st) 6 times [18]

Rnd 4: (sc 2, 2 sc in next st) 6 times [24]

Rnd 5: (sc 3, 2 sc in next st) 6 times [30]

Rnd 6: (sc 4, 2 sc in next st) 6 times, turn [36]

The next section is worked back and forth in rows to create the split for the lilypad.

Row 7: ch 1, (sc 5, 2 sc in next st) 5 times, sc 6, turn [41]

Row 8: ch 1, (sc 6, 2 sc in next st) 5 times, sc 6, turn [46]

Row 9: ch 1, (sc 7, 2 sc in next st) 5 times, sc 6, turn [51]

Row 10: ch 1, (sc 8, 2 sc in next st) 5 times, sc 6, turn [56]

Row 11: ch 1, (sc 9, 2 sc in next st) 5 times, sc 6, turn [61]

Row 12: ch 1, (sc 10, 2 sc in next st) 5 times, sc 6, do NOT turn [66]

Rnd 13: sl st in each st around including the "V" created in the lilypad

Invisible fasten off and weave in ends. Attach to the water.

WATER LILY

Rnd 1: with **2.5mm** hook and **yellow DK** yarn, sc 8 in magic ring [8]

Rnd 2: working in FLO, (sl st 1, ch 4, sl st in 2nd ch from hook, sl st in next 2 ch sts) 8 times, sl st [32]

Rnd 3: working in BLO from **Rnd 1**, 2 sc in each st around [16]

Rnd 4: working in FLO from **Rnd 3**, (sl st 1, ch 5, sl st in 2nd ch from hook, sl st in next 3 ch sts) 16 times, sl st [80]

Rnd 5: join **white DK** yarn, working in BLO from **Rnd 3**, (2 sc in next st, sc 1) 8 times [24]

Rnd 6: working in FLO from **Rnd 5**, (sc 1, ch 5, sl st in 2nd ch from hook, sc in next ch st, hdc in next ch st, dc in next ch st, hdc in same st as first sc made, sl st 1, sc 1) 8 times [64]

Rnd 7: working in BLO from **Rnd 5**, (2 sc in next st, sc 2) 8 times [32]

Rnd 8: working in FLO from **Rnd 7**, (sc 1, ch 6, sl st in 2nd ch from hook, sc in next ch st, hdc in next ch st, dc in next ch st, tr in next ch st, dc in same st as first sc made, skip 1, sl st 1, sc 1) 8 times [72]

Rnd 9: working in BLO from **Rnd 7**, (2 sc in next st, sc 3) 8 times [40]

Rnd 10: working in FLO from **Rnd 9**, (sc 3, ch 8, sl st in 2nd ch from hook, sl st in next 6 ch sts, sl st in same st as first sc made, sc 2) 8 times [104]

In **Rnd 11** you will be working around the 8 foundation chains created in **Rnd 10**.

Rnd 11: (sl st 2, tr 2, dc 2, hdc 1, sc 1, sl st 1, ch 1, sl st 1, sc 1, hdc 1, dc 2, tr 2, skip next 2 sts, sl st 1) repeat 8 times [144]

Fasten off and weave in ends.

Attach the water lily to the lilypad.

TECHNIQUES

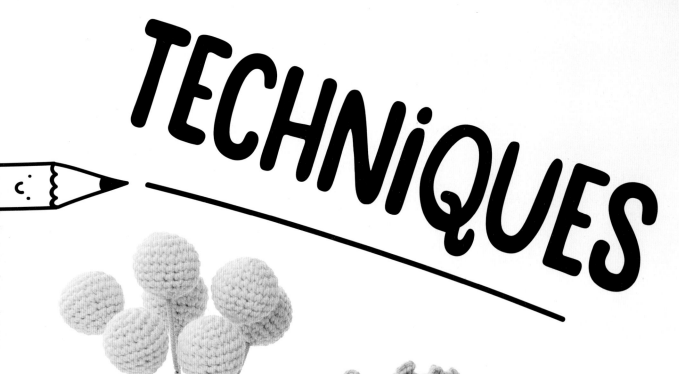

USEFUL INFORMATION

Key to Pattern Charts

▷   Starting Point

○   Chain

●   Slip Stitch

×   Single Crochet

丅   Half Double Crochet

𝈋   Double Crochet

𝈋   Treble Crochet

Terminology

All of the patterns in this book are written using US crochet terms.

Conversion Chart (US to UK)

- Single Crochet (sc) = Double Crochet (dc)
- Double Crochet (dc) = Treble Crochet (tr)
- Half Double Crochet (hdc) = Half Treble Crochet (htr)
- Treble Crochet (tr) = Double Treble Crochet (dtr)

Pattern Abbreviations

- 3-dc-bl = 3 double crochet bobble
- BLO = back loops only
- ch = chain stitch
- ch-2 picot = chain 2 picot
- dc = double crochet stitch
- FLO = front loops only
- hdc = half double crochet
- rnd = round
- sc = single crochet stitch
- sc2tog = single crochet decrease
- sl st = slip stitch
- st(s) = stitch(es)
- tr = treble crochet stitch
- scSP-1 = single crochet spike stitch one row down between sl st and st(s)

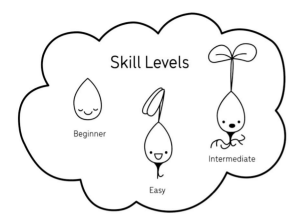

Skill Levels

Beginner

Easy

Intermediate

How to Read Patterns

- Abbreviations are used throughout the book, please see Pattern Abbreviations to see how stitches are described.

- Almost all patterns are worked in a continuous spiral; you only need to join a round if the pattern specifically instructs you to.

- If something is crocheted in rows it will begin with Row instead of Rnd.

- Repetitions throughout the round are placed in parentheses, and the number of times this part is repeated is added behind the parentheses. For example, **(sc 2, 2 sc in next st) 6 times**. This means to crochet 1 single crochet stitch over the first 2 stitches, then make 2 single crochet stitches (or a single crochet increase) in the third stitch, next the sequence of 1 single crochet in the next 2 stitches and 2 single crochet stitches in the next stitch is repeated another 5 times.

- A sequence of stitches worked in the same stitch is joined with a +. For example, **(sl st + ch 2 + dc 1 + ch 2 + sl st) 4 times**. This means crochet a slip stitch, chain 2, 1 double crochet, chain 2, and a slip stitch all in the next stitch and then repeat the sequence another 3 times.

- At the end of each line you will find the total number of stitches you should have in square brackets, for example, **[24]** means you have should have 24 total stitches in that round or row once complete.

Modifying the Design

The easiest way to make your amigurumi unique is by selecting a different yarn weight to the one the pattern calls for.

For example, if you wish to make a giant Ladybug cushion you could use a bulky weight yarn and the amigurumi will be larger, while maintaining the same proportions. Or, if you wish to make a tiny Caterpillar keychain, you could select a fingering weight yarn and a smaller hook size. The wonderful thing about amigurumi is that when the yarn weight and corresponding hook size is changed the proportions still remain the same!

If changing the yarn weight you'll need to change the hook size too. Always choose a slightly smaller hook size than the recommended size on the label band of your yarn. This helps to keep the stitches tight enough to prevent the fabric from having large stretch holes when it's stuffed.

BASIC STITCHES

Magic Ring

With the tail end of the yarn hanging down, make a loop and hold it securely between two fingers (1).

Insert the hook into the loop and pull the working yarn through (2), make a chain stitch to secure, and begin making stitches inside the loop (3). When you've finished, pull the tail to tighten the loop.

Slip Knot

Make a loop with the tail end of the yarn hanging down. Insert the hook or your fingers into the loop and pull the working yarn through (4). Pull to tighten.

Chain (ch)

Place the yarn over the hook and pull through the loop (5).

Slip Stitch (sl st)

Insert the hook into the stitch, place the yarn over the hook, and pull through the stitch and loop on the hook (6).

Single Crochet (sc)

Insert the hook into the stitch, place the yarn over the hook, and pull through the stitch, so that two loops are on the hook (7). Place the yarn over the hook again and pull through both loops on the hook (8).

Half Double Crochet (hdc)

Place the yarn over the hook and insert the hook into the stitch (9). Yarn over and pull through the stitch. Place the yarn over the hook again and pull through all three loops on the hook (10).

Double Crochet (dc)

Place the yarn over the hook and insert the hook into the stitch (11). Yarn over and pull through the stitch, so that three loops are left on the hook. Yarn over and pull through the first two loops on the hook, so that two loops are left on the hook (12). Yarn over and pull through the remaining two loops.

Treble Crochet (tr)

Place the yarn over the hook twice and insert the hook into the stitch (13). Yarn over and pull through the stitch. Yarn over and pull through the first two loops on the hook, so that there are three loops left on the hook (14). Yarn over and pull through the first two loops on the hook again, so that there are two loops left on the hook. Yarn over again and pull through the remaining two loops.

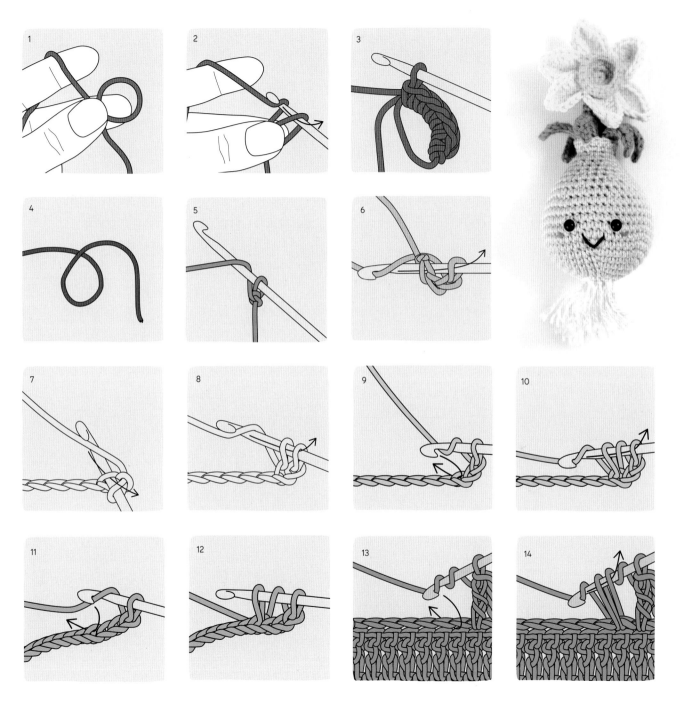

OTHER STITCHES

Invisible Single Crochet Decrease

The standard method of decreasing can leave a small gap or bump when making a three-dimensional piece. Using the invisible single crochet decrease when making amigurumi results in a smoother and more even fabric.

Insert the hook into the front loop of the first stitch and then directly into the front loop of the second stitch, place the yarn over the hook (1), and draw the yarn through both of the front loops on your hook, two loops are now on the hook. Place the yarn over the hook again and draw the yarn through both loops on your hook to finish a single crochet stitch (2).

This also works for taller stitches such as hdc or dc decreases.

Standard Single Crochet Decrease (sc2tog)

Insert the hook into the first stitch, place the yarn over the hook, and pull a loop through the stitch, two loops are now on the hook (3). Insert the hook into the second stitch, place the yarn over the hook, and pull a loop through the stitch, three loops are now on the hook (4). Place the yarn over the hook and pull through all three loops on the hook.

Chain-2 Picot (ch-2 picot)

Chain 2, slip stitch in 2nd ch from hook

3-Double Crochet Bobble (3-dc-bl)

Place the yarn over the hook and insert the hook into the stitch, yarn over and pull the yarn through the stitch, yarn over and draw yarn through the first two loops on the hook, two loops are now on the hook.

Yarn over and insert hook into the same stitch. Yarn over and pull the yarn through the stitch. Yarn over and draw yarn through the first two loops on the hook, three loops are now on the hook.

Repeat the last step until you have four loops on the hook (5). Yarn over and pull the yarn through all four loops on the hook. Make a chain to secure the stitch (6).

Single Crochet Spike Stitch-One Row Down (scSP-1)

This is also called a Long Single Crochet.

Insert the hook from front to back into the space between stitches directly one row below. Draw the yarn through the stitch and up to the current level of work. Yarn over and draw the yarn through two loops on the hook.

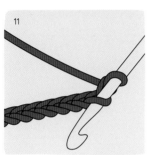

Right Side / Wrong Side of Crocheted Fabric

When crocheting in rounds it's important to be able to distinguish which side of the crocheted piece is the right side. This is especially true when you are asked to work in the front or back loops of a stitch.

On the right or front side there are little "V"s that appear (7). The wrong or back side has horizontal lines which are called back bumps or back bars (8).

Back Bump / Back Bar

The back bump or back bar can be found on the 'wrong side' of the fabric and lies right below the back loop of a stitch (7 and 8).

Back Bump / Back Bar of a Foundation Chain

On the front or right side of your crochet chain, the stitches are smooth and look like a series of interlocking "V"s (9). On the back or wrong side, the stitches are bumpy.

Crocheting in the back bumps along a chain creates a neater finish (10).

Front Loop (FLO)

The front loop of a stitch is the loop closest to you. If the crochet pattern says to work in front loops only (FLO) you will work your stitches into just this front loop (11).

Back Loop (BLO)

The back loop is the loop furthest away from you. If the crochet pattern says to work in back loops only (BLO) you will work your stitches into just this back loop (12).

COLORWORK

Changing Colors

The color change method used throughout this book is to change the color in the last step of the previous stitch. Start the previous stitch as usual, but when completing the last yarn over pull through the new color (1). Drop the old yarn color and continue making the next stitch with the new color (2 and 3).

Joining Yarn

Insert the hook into the indicated stitch, wrap the yarn around the hook and pull it through the stitch, yarn over the hook, and pull through to secure (4).

Carrying Yarn / Crocheting With Two Colors

Carrying the yarn means you don't have to fasten the yarn off and rejoin a new strand each time you make a color change. This technique is helpful when making the Caterpillar pattern because a color change is made every few rounds.

There are various methods for doing this but carrying the yarn up at the beginning of each round is the technique used in this book. To do this, change the yarn color in the last step of the previous stitch (see Changing Colors) by simply letting the current color drop and by picking up the new color.

FINISHING

Fasten Off

Cut the yarn and pull the yarn tail through the last loop on your hook.

Invisible Fasten Off

When you fasten off invisibly you get a smooth even edge. Cut the yarn and pull the yarn tail through the last stitch. Thread the yarn tail onto a yarn needle, insert the needle, from front to back, into the next stitch. Now insert the needle back into the same stitch that the yarn tail is coming out of, but into the back loop only, and pull gently (5). Weave the tail end into the wrong side of the fabric and cut the excess (6).

Weave In Ends As You Go

When changing colors with a three-dimensional piece, you can weave in the initial yarn tail of the new color and the remaining yarn tail of the previous color as you go by "carrying" both yarn tails. To do this, lay both yarn tails along the edge on top of the stitches to be worked and crochet over the strands for the next five to six stitches.

Keep the carried strand of yarn tight enough so that it lies flat against the wrong side of the fabric and doesn't catch on anything, but don't pull the strand too tight or the fabric will pucker.

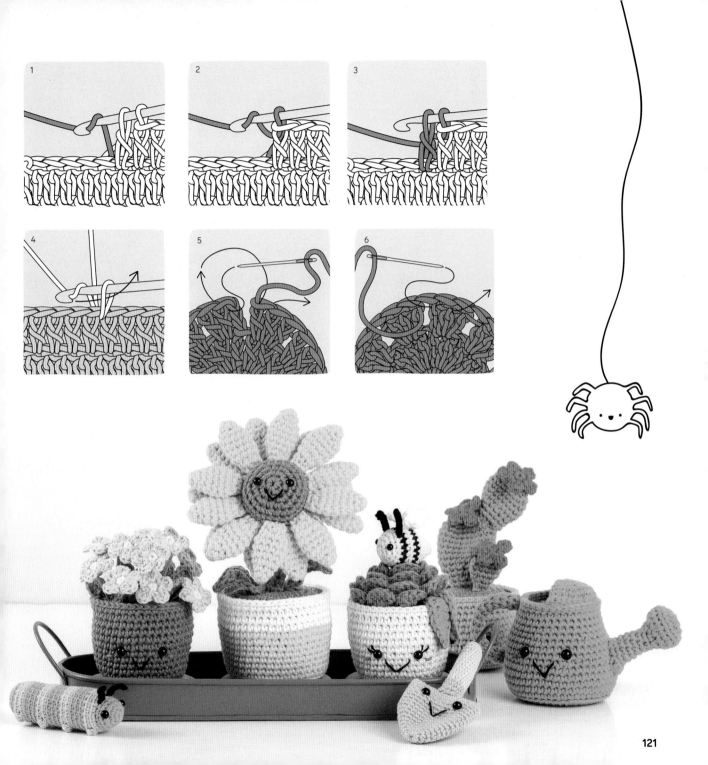

MAKING UP

The same technique applies when closing through the back loops. You will just be inserting your needle in the back loops instead of the front loops as described.

Inserting Safety Eyes

Safety Note: Do not use toy safety eyes if giving to a child under three years of age. Instead, use black yarn to embroider the eyes.

Each pattern indicates which rows or rounds the safety eyes should be placed in and how many stitches there should be between them. Make sure you are happy with the placement of the safety eyes before inserting the washer onto the rod of the eye because once the washer is placed you won't be able to pull it off again.

Stuffing

Stuffing a piece firmly, but not so much that the stuffing shows between the stitches, is my secret to knowing how much fiberfill stuffing to use.

Closing Stitches Through Front Loops

Cut the yarn and pull the yarn tail through the last stitch. Thread onto a yarn needle. Insert the needle through the front loops only of each of the remaining stitches from inside to outside (1 and 2). Pull gently to close the hole (3). Insert the needle in the center of the stitches you just closed and come out in any direction from the middle of the crocheted piece (4). Tie a knot close to the amigurumi and push the knot inside the crocheted piece. Cut the excess yarn tail.

Crocheting Two Pieces Together

Line up the stitches from both rounds that need to be crocheted together by placing one round of stitches on top of the other (5). With the yarn that has not been fastened off from one of the crochet pieces, single crochet around the entire piece working in both loops of both pieces to join them together (6).

Shaping

Shaping makes it possible for these kawaii characters to stand up straight on a flat surface. The goal while shaping, unless otherwise instructed in a pattern, is to create an indentation at the bottom of the amigurumi, but none at the top.

Begin shaping by inserting the needle from the center bottom of a crocheted piece to the center top (7 and 8). Take the needle back down from the center top to slightly off the center bottom (9 and 10). Take the needle back up from the center bottom to the center top (11). Pull to create an indentation in the bottom of the crocheted piece (12). There should be no indentation in the top (13). Take the needle back down the center from the top to the bottom. Secure the yarn with two or three knots and weave in the ends.

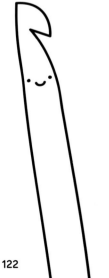

Fastening Off Inside a Three-Dimensional Piece

With the yarn tail threaded in a yarn needle, insert the needle through the entire middle of the crochet piece. Tie a knot close to the amigurumi and push the knot inside the crocheted piece. Cut any excess yarn tail.

Yarn-Wrapped Stem

Cut a piece of 20-gauge floral wire 10cm (4in) long (1). Place a drop of hot glue on one end of the wire. Begin wrapping with **green DK** yarn (2). Wrap yarn around the entire length of the wire, then apply another drop of hot glue at the end (3 and 4).

Yarn-Wrapped Blossom Stem

Take a yarn-wrapped stem and bend one end of the wire around a crochet hook to create a circle (5 and 6). Bend the long end of the wire down to create a flat surface for the blossom to be attached (7 and 8).

Crocheting with Floral Wire

Cut wire to the length specified in the pattern. Hold the wire behind the foundation chain of stitches (9). Insert your hook into the chain stitch and under the wire. Crochet stitches as normal; doing so will cause the yarn to wrap around the wire as you crochet (10 and 11).

Stitching Facial Details

With **black** yarn, insert the yarn needle in the amigurumi at any point in the back and stitch on a "V" for the mouth. The mouth should be placed in the center between the eyes and almost the same height as the eyes, but one round down (12 and 13).

With the desired cheek color, insert the yarn needle in the amigurumi at any point in the back (14). Stitch on cheeks on either side of the eyes and almost the same width as the eyes, but one round down (15 and 16).

After stitching on both cheeks, insert the needle through the entire middle of the crochet piece. Tie a knot close to the amigurumi and push the knot inside the crocheted piece. Cut any excess yarn tail.

When stitching on eyelashes, I find it easiest to use a double strand of sewing thread and a sewing needle. This makes it easier to work close to the safety eye and insert the needle at any point in the fabric.

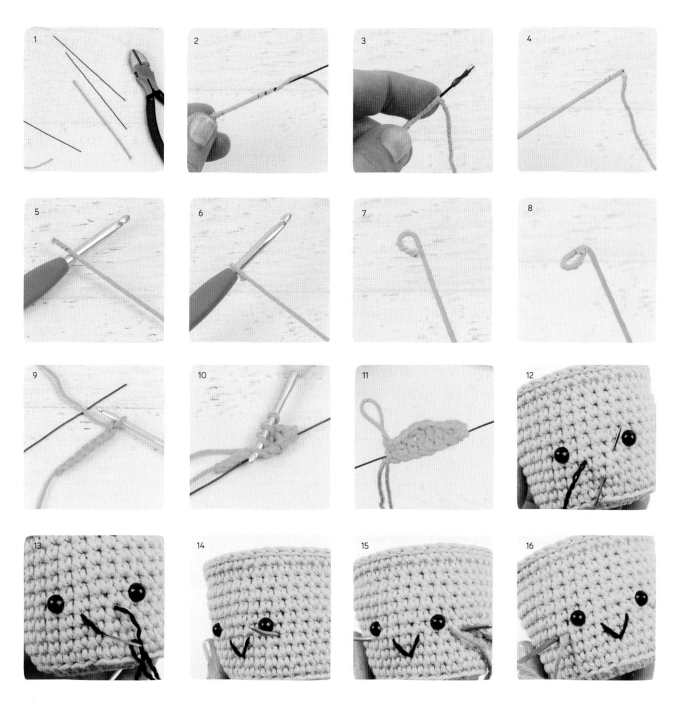

#kawaiicrochet

ABOUT THE AUTHOR

Melissa Bradley is a crochet designer and color enthusiast who has a love for all things handmade. She has a bachelor's degree in interior design and is a certified florist, but it was after the birth of her second child that she fell in love with a new medium of design: yarn. If she doesn't have a crochet hook in hand, she can be found baking or out in the garden. You can find her patterns on Etsy, Ravelry, and LoveCrochet. She lives in Utah, USA.

ACKNOWLEDGMENTS

First, I want to say thank you to all the makers who have supported my crochet journey over the years. For everyone who supported *Kawaii Crochet* and was thrilled and excited for its sequel. Thank you!

Also, a huge thank you to the lovely and talented team at David & Charles. Thank you, Ame Verso, for believing in me, yet again, and letting me be my best creative self. Thank you to Jeni Chown, Sam Staddon, Lucy Waldron, Anna Wade, Prudence Rogers, and Jason Jenkins. It has been such a joy and privilege to work with so many talented individuals on the making of this book.

I am also incredibly grateful and would like to thank my family. For my children who have so patiently waited for me to stop counting stitches in my head before I answered a question or who waited to go do something "fun" after I finished just "one more round". Thank you for your love and support! You are the light of my life and are always the inspiration behind my creations.

Most importantly, I need to express my gratitude to my parents for their unfailing support during the making of this book. These pages were only completed because of their listening ears and endless love. I am truly at a loss for words when it comes to expressing my gratitude for you both during this time in my life. Thank you and I love you!

INDEX

A DAVID AND CHARLES BOOK
© David and Charles, Ltd 2022

David and Charles is an imprint of David and Charles, Ltd
Suite A, Tourism House, Pynes Hill, Exeter, EX2 5WS

Text and Designs © Melissa Bradley 2022
Layout and Photography © David and Charles, Ltd 2022

First published in the UK and USA in 2022

A catalogue record for this book is available from the British Library.

ISBN-13: 9781446309063 paperback
ISBN-13: 9781446381380 EPUB
ISBN-13: 9781446381373 PDF

This book has been printed on paper from approved suppliers and made from pulp from sustainable sources.

Printed in China by Asia Pacific Offset for:
David and Charles, Ltd
Suite A, Tourism House, Pynes Hill, Exeter, EX2 5WS

10 9 8 7 6 5

Publishing Director: Ame Verso
Managing Editor: Jeni Chown
Project Editor: Sarah Hoggett
Technical Editor: Sharon Carter
Head of Design: Sam Staddon
Designers: Anna Wade and Lucy Waldron
Pre-press Designer: Ali Stark
Art Direction: Prudence Rogers
Photography: Jason Jenkins
Photo editing: Nick Leggett
Production Manager: Beverley Richardson

David and Charles publishes high-quality books on a wide range of subjects. For more information visit www.davidandcharles.com.

Share your makes with us on social media using #dandcbooks and follow us on Facebook and Instagram by searching for @dandcbooks.

Layout of the digital edition of this book may vary depending on reader hardware and display settings.